D1453157

From
My Old Kentucky Home
to
The White House

FROM
MY OLD KENTUCKY HOME
TO
THE WHITE HOUSE

The Political Journey

of

Catherine Conner

Catherine Conner

THE UNIVERSITY PRESS OF KENTUCKY

Copyright © 1999 by The University Press of Kentucky

Scholarly publisher for the Commonwealth,
serving Bellarmine College, Berea College, Centre
College of Kentucky, Eastern Kentucky University,
The Filson Club Historical Society, Georgetown College,
Kentucky Historical Society, Kentucky State University,
Morehead State University, Murray State University,
Northern Kentucky University, Transylvania University,
University of Kentucky, University of Louisville,
and Western Kentucky University.

Editorial and Sales Offices: The University Press of Kentucky
663 South Limestone Street, Lexington, Kentucky 40508-4008

03 02 01 00 99   5 4 3 2 1

Library of Congress Cataloging-in-Publication Data

Conner, Catherine, 1900-
    From my old Kentucky home to the White House : the political
journey of Catherine Conner / Catherine Conner.
        p.   cm.
    Includes index.
    ISBN 0-8131-2102-7 (cloth : alk. paper)
    1. Conner, Catherine, 1900-   . 2. Women politicians—
Kentucky—Biography. 3. Politicians—Kentucky—Biography.
4. Kentucky—Politics and government—1865-1950. 5. Kentucky—
Politics and government—1951-   6. United States—Politics and
government—1933-1945. 7. United States—Politics and government—
1945-1989. 8. Bullitt County (Ky.)—Biography. I. Title.
F456.C75   1999
973.91'092—dc21   98-49706
[B]

This book is printed on acid-free recycled paper
meeting the requirements of the American National Standard
for Permanence of Paper for Printed Library Materials.

Manufactured in the United States of America

Contents

Illustrations follow page 86

Those who flow as life flows, know
They need no other force;
They feel no wear, they feel no tear,
They need no mending, no repair.

—Catherine Conner

Preface

As TAGORE SAID, "Faith is the bird that feels the light and sings when the dawn is still dark." So did my family. I have written this book as a legacy, to the memory of my only son and as a tribute to my two living grandsons, who have coaxed me to "tell it all." Telling it all is not that easy—not because I don't remember but because there have been bruised times as well as wonderful times.

What follows is not just a string of anecdotes. I believe that incidents I recall from my life, especially my Washington years, evoke people, crises, and triumphs of a time long gone. Historians—the real ones—try to knit together what happened. In a modest way, this work can add a footnote to their research.

It is a long way from a Kentucky farm to Chicago, to Washington, D.C., to New York, to California, to Europe, and back to Kentucky. Along the way there were husbands, dear friends, and bums. There were both triumphs and tragedies.

I recall my childhood as being wonderful. The thousand-acre farm at Solitude, in Bullitt County, Kentucky, where I used to live, might seem like something out of an old Shirley Temple movie—with a few rude incidents added.

My strong, strapping father, a great horseman and a great companion to all, introduced my mornings with what he called a "toddy"—milk laced with bourbon. My wonderful mother brought down fire and brimstone on the practice. (More than ninety years later I still do not mind a bourbon or two with friends.)

As the years went on and Catholic school came and went—after a winding road, I am still devout in my fashion—I married and had a child, then almost accidentally came upon the springboard that launched me into the stories I have to tell. That springboard was politics.

1

Solitude

MY PERSONAL HISTORY BEGAN in February 1898, when my
mother, Nancy Barbee Hayes, married my father, James
Valandingham Rouse, at the old Galt House in Louisville,
Kentucky. Following the ceremony on that bitterly cold day,
they went to the wharf at the foot of Fourth Street to board a
boat on which they floated down the Ohio River to the Mis-
sissippi; and, after several days, to a festive and warm New
Orleans. At the end of the honeymoon they returned on the
boat to Louisville, where they were met by Mama's brother
with a beautiful carriage and a spanking pair of matched
bays. The carriage and horses were Mama's wedding gift
from her family. He then drove them out to Solitude, my
father's farm some thirty miles south of Louisville in Bullitt
County.

I was born in 1900; and while I was a little girl, my mother
painted for me word pictures of the early days in that part of
Kentucky. Roads were nothing more than buffalo trails criss-
crossing from county to county, occasionally connecting with
fairly good roads known as turnpikes, free paved roads that
had formerly been toll roads. Even these turnpikes were primi-
tive, just wide enough for the passing of wagons, buggies, or
carriages.

Solitude consisted of some one thousand acres spread between low hills. A creek ran through the farm that in the spring overflowed the low–lying corn lands, which were referred to as the bottoms. On this farm lived my father's mother and father, his brother and his family, and three tenant farmers.

My father's father was also named James Valandingham Rouse, and his father was James Anderson Rouse, the Anderson from his mother, Ann Anderson, who was from Scotland. (Scots frugality was a trait all the way down to my father.) Great–grandfather came from the Netherlands, where the family was Von Rouse. When he came to America, he dropped the Von, which infuriated his family. When his father died, he was left only eighty pieces of silver. He had them beaten into a large silver ladle, which he presented to his wife, Mitilda Petticord, as a wedding present. Today, this beautiful, rare piece belongs to my grandson Sam Conner.

My grandmother Rouse was born Martha Ann Wells. She came of a slave–owning family, and her wedding present had been slaves. She was tiny with keen blue eyes that could snap with anger or soften with sympathy. With the approach of the War Between the States, my grandfather tried to recruit white workers for the farm and free their slaves, my grandmother became incensed because they were "her property," and she conceived a hatred of Abraham Lincoln. A meticulous housekeeper and famous cook, she ruled her household with an iron hand.

Mama's family was from Lexington, where her great–grandfather John Bradford had started the first newspaper in Kentucky in 1787.

Our own beautiful house topped a small rise overlooking the entire valley. Between two hills in a hollow nestled the family distillery. The whiskey was called Old Mellwood and was made for the benefit and joy of those who lived on the farm, as well as near neighbors.

There were no phones in the entire valley and surrounding territory. All communications were delivered on horseback. To contact the nearest doctor, a rider had to be dispatched ten miles or so. The doctor usually arrived by buggy some ten or twelve hours later, often at midnight or four o'clock in the morning, or whenever he could make it. Those wonderful men traveled over rough roads, barely paths, day and night, giving aid and comfort to the ill.

When anyone in our neighborhood became seriously ill, Mama was always sent for to help until the doctor arrived. Her mother was from Lexington, Kentucky, where her father and brothers raised blooded horses, so Mama loved horses and rode side saddle, occasionally accompanying my father on his long rides over the farm.

Mama told me about home remedies concocted from roots, berries, and plants, which she learned from the offspring of the Indians who had roamed these hills and valleys some one hundred years before her time. She always said most of the ills we suffer today would have been overlooked in her younger days.

My father, always an enterprising man, began the work of getting landowners to contribute so many days a year for the building of roads, which were necessary to connect their farms to the stock market in Louisville. The Louisville & National Railroad was only ten miles away, but transportation to and from the railroad was so bad that most of the farmers preferred to haul by wagon to the turnpike leading into Louisville, a trip that took at least two days. The neighbors agreed to my father's proposal. After the roads were built through the woods to the railways, farmers found they could deliver twice as many products as formerly and the trip took only four hours.

Papa also saw the need for mail delivery to the communities. He went to Washington, D.C., and finally got a post office established in the local store. Mail time was a convenient time for neighbors to meet and discuss the business of the week. What the pubs were to Ireland and England, the local post office was to rural America. These meetings usually took place when the once–a–week mail was delivered on Saturday morning. But in spring, summer, and fall, everyone was too busy to spend much time gossiping. So the church—in our case, the Baptist Church—was the gossip grounds on Sundays. Going to church was not only doing God's work but also a social event.

The post office was the source of great pleasure to my father because he valued the newspapers that enabled him to keep up with the markets and world events. Though not an educated man in the usual sense, he had nevertheless read all the books in his grandfather's extensive library, which included the works of Dickens and Shakespeare. He also knew the Bible from cover to cover. He was also a good farmer and an adequate architect in that he knew how to build houses, barns, and fences and do general repairs.

The farm was almost completely self–supporting. The only things we bought were tea, coffee, salt, black pepper, sugar, and once a year a barrel of blackstrap molasses that came from New Orleans. We had our own water–ground cornmeal and flour ground in our own mills. In winter, great slabs of ice were cut from the creek and stored in an icehouse built two–thirds underground and filled with sawdust from our sawmill. In the icehouse went great crocks of milk, butter, watermelons, and kegs of beer. Copper beer mugs hung on the icehouse wall. The buying of beer was my father's one extravagance. In the summer he loved to come home after hours of hot work on the farm and have a good cold mug of beer before and during his supper. He always said it was better then than whiskey—whiskey being the winter drink. The ice was never used in drinking water or cooking water. Papa was afraid of typhoid fever and other illnesses caused by germs that might be in the creek. Our all–purpose water came from cisterns of rainwater filtered through charcoal. It was always fresh and cold.

We had orchards of apple, plum, cherry, and pear trees and a grape arbor. How I loved that grape arbor! There was a wooden seat at the end of it where I used to sit in the long summer evenings eating grapes and dreaming of the world beyond the hills of our farm. There was also a huge garden that supplied vegetables enough for the summer and later to can and put on shelves in the large, cool cellar that ran the entire length of our house. Sauerkraut was made in kegs and stored there. There was also a root cellar where turnips, parsnips, onions, potatoes, and pumpkins were stored. Large boxes of black walnuts and hickory nuts were gathered to use in cakes, pies and salads. Mint and watercress grew around the icehouse in abundant profusion. The chicken and turkey yards supplied our eggs and poultry, and the fall was hog–killing season.

How well I remember hog–killing time. When I was four years old, my father had given me a tiny white pig—the runt of the litter—for a pet. I fed that little pig, washed her, took her for walks, and kept her in a box by my bed. She was beautiful, so pink and white, and so intelligent. She seemed to understand every word I said. If she were snoozing by the kitchen stove on a cold afternoon and I called, "Come on, Katy" (I named her after myself; but as I was always called Catherine, I believed no one knew), she would come grunting and wiggling her tiny tail, trotting beside me into the snow or blustery cold. We would race, and her short little legs would pound along until we were both breathless.

She grew and grew, and one day Papa took her out to the pig yard where he said she belonged with her brothers and sisters. I was lonely for her, but my father's word was law. In the night I heard a wild squealing that I recognized as Katy's. I jumped out of bed and on that cold night; and by the light of a faint moon, I saw Katy trying desperately to get away from the other hogs in the pig yard. Racing to her, I opened the gate and called out, "Katy! Here, Katy!" She rushed to me and kept making toneless little grunts as I gathered her in my arms. A big old hog that looked like a giant to me rushed at us. I got Katy through the gate and slammed it into the hog's charging face. He squalled and tried to pull his snout out of the wire gate, but it was stuck. I picked up a plank and smacked him full in the snout.

Katy and I made it back to the kitchen where I drew a bucket of water and washed her clean again. All the time she snuggled up to me and made pitiful little grunts. I put her box behind the stove and lay down beside her. Finally, I heard a faint little snore and knew Katy was settled and asleep. I tried sleeping on the cold floor, but it was impossible. I crept up the stairs for blankets; but when I left the kitchen, Katy sensed it and began to make her pitiful little grunts again. I rushed to my room gathering up blankets and dragged them down the steps. But Papa had heard us; and as I sat by Katy's box, I saw a light coming through the dining room.

At the door, my father's voice thundered, "Who's there?"

I said nothing; but Katy, accustomed to the familiar voice, grunted plaintively.

"How in hell did she get in here?" Papa was looking down at Katy and me. "Come on, Catherine, go back to bed."

I left her curled up and went back upstairs to bed.

It was late the next morning when I awakened; and hearing the noise from the slaughter pen, I rushed down the stairs and out of the house. There, to my horror, I saw Katy slaughtered and split wide open. I screamed and screamed for hours until the doctor arrived and put me to sleep.

When I came to, Papa told me it had been an accident. One of the hands had shot her by mistake. I never believed him; nor, deep in my heart, did I ever forgive him. Katy, my pink and white baby, had been brutally murdered. It was a long time before I could touch pork again, and I could never look at the round brick house where hams, sausages, spare-ribs, and backbones were hung to cure for six weeks over slow–burning hickory logs without a general sickness of my stomach.

2

Jenny

THERE WERE THE THREE OF US—Mama, Papa, and me. But most of all there was Papa. Six feet tall and just under 160 pounds, he had piercing green eyes, black hair, and strong, prominent features, doubtless from some distant Irish ancestor. I used to love to roll his name off my tongue, "James Valandingham Rouse."

A prince on a white charger was what Papa was to me. I took this image from a picture in a childhood storybook from which he used to read to me. When supper was finished, he would pull a chair up to the table and turn the lamp high. Then he would take me on his knee and begin: "Once upon a time. . . ."

From time to time, he would stop reading and press a long finger to the page with the picture of the white horse that performed such feats as swimming a swift creek with a little girl on his back or galloping miles uphill and down with a note to the doctor tied to his bridle. Always there were my questions. How did the horse have enough strength to swim with a girl on his back? How did the horse know where the doctor lived?

"Because, Cathy, he was a white charger," Papa always replied.

Papa's real horse was a bay named Ed. No one on the farm except Papa could ride the fiery little stallion, a feat that was a great source of pride to him. Papa loved to play poker, drink bourbon, and ride Ed; those were his three loves. Yet he always assured me that he loved me most of all, I sometimes doubted when I watched him drink his old–fashioned with such gusto, or jump on Ed for a long gallop.

I remember standing at the window watching him gallop down the drive on Ed. I would run out, begging for a ride. The tension ran high between Papa, Ed, and me. Ed was determined not to let Papa take me up on his back. I can see that horse now, dancing sideways, snorting, ready to bolt, and Papa sitting very still in the saddle, a stern, steady hand on the bridle. He would be cursing softly under his breath. But I was too busy to hear exactly what he was saying because I had to be very careful to be ready at just the right moment when he would swoop down from the saddle and make a grab for me. I held my breath then, just as Ed seemed to do. After Papa had swung me high over the saddle and settled me in front of him, he would give the crop a snap, and we were off. With a loud snort and a quick jump, Ed would run faster and faster beneath the reins whipping in Papa's hands.

Grandma Rouse would see us go by sometimes; and when she'd get me alone she'd say, with an ominous shake of her head, "You and your father are going to be killed on that horse some day, you and your father laughing and hollering and that fool horse running as if the devil was after him."

Papa, Ed, and I loved those rides. It was the only real excitement we had, and I have never known a thrill to compare to those wild rides we used to have.

A typical day with Papa began with an early morning visit, an awakening kiss, and the familiar cream toddy. He would offer me a sip and I would always accept, not understanding what the ingredients were. "Whiskey" was a household word. When men came to visit, Papa would say, "Let's have a whiskey," or "Why isn't the whiskey on the sideboard?" if he ever wanted some and the jug was missing. I knew it was whiskey, but that knowledge had no significance for me. I only knew that I loved the stuff that came out of the brown jug. How hungry it made me every morning!

I remember well the fuss Mama made early one morning when she came into my room and discovered what it was I was being fed for breakfast. Clapping a hand over her mouth to stifle a scream, she yelled, "How dare you! How dare you!"

"Just a spoonful of cream and sugar," Papa said as she grabbed the glass out of his hand and, running to the window, threw the toddy into the yard. He did not say another word because his jaw was set tight and his face had grown red, a strong face that could flash thunder and lightning when he was crossed. His eyes narrowed in anger and he left the room muttering something about "that fool woman." When he was gone, I remember, I cried. Even then, child that I was, I had sensed his hurt.

Later, when people would comment on my healthy appearance, Papa would tell them that it was due to the early morning breakfast he fed me. Then, when neighboring women asked what the breakfast consisted of, he would smile and say, "Just a little something, a secret between Cath and me."

One morning I awakened, somewhat surprised that Papa had not come in with my early breakfast (as we called it after the time Mama caught us). The house was quiet, and I lay a moment listening to its emptiness. But I could hear something out in the back yard. Someone was crying. Jumping out of bed and stepping into my slippers and dress, I ran toward the kitchen.

The kitchen, which was separated from the main house by a porch, was deserted. This was unusual because Lou, my lovely black Mammy, was always at the stove this time of morning. It was seven o'clock (a fact that I know well because I had just learned to tell time that week). Lou should have been cooking breakfast, but the stove was cold.

I stopped and listened. Yes, it was sobbing I heard. Then I heard Lou and Mama talking. Instinct told me something was wrong, very wrong. I tiptoed to the back porch, looked out, and saw Mama, Lou, and Lou's daughter, Jenny, standing at the foot of the steps.

Jenny was a big, strapping tomboy who used to ride me around on her back in the orchard in summer so that I could reach up and get the ripe, sun–warmed apples from the trees. Then we would have what Jenny, who was tongue–tied, called a "pithnic." I had thought nothing of it when Bill Jones, one of the tenants living on the place, began to join us on our "pithnics." I would wait impatiently while Bill and Jenny ran off into the big weeds, to "play," as they always said.

One day I followed them and peeped through the bushes. I saw them "playing" in a most peculiar way. They heard me; and while Jenny got into her clothes, Bill twisted my arm until I fell to the ground crying with pain. He kept muttering, "If you ever tell, I'll kill you!" He had such a look on his face that I believed him.

Finally, Jenny came out of the bushes. She was mad and called me "Meddlesome Mattie," a name I took to be something terrible, and I cried even louder.

"Black bitch!" Bill yelled at Jenny. "Take that crybaby home. If either one of you ever says anything about this, I'll kill both of you!" Then he stalked off down through the orchard with his head hanging.

I watched his big, dirty white feet moving through the grass. When he was gone I sobbed, "I'm going to tell Papa, Jenny. He can't talk to me like that, to you either, or play like that."

But Jenny, crying too, picked me up and, putting me on her back for the ride to the house, said, "No, honey, don't say nothin'. I's black and he's white. If anybody found out, them white men 'ud beat me to death—and so would Mammy," she added, still crying.

Jenny

I didn't see much of Jenny for a while after that last "pithnic," so I was glad to see her standing there that morning. But she was crying again, just as she had that day in the orchard. Her sobbing brought back that awful scene with Bill Jones, a scene I had not been able to forget.

As I listened, I heard Lou say to Mama, "I tell you, Ma'am, she gonna have a baby, 'n I'm gonna have his name outen her if I has to beat her to death." Then, turning to Jenny, she screamed, "You hear me, black gal?"

Jenny cried louder than ever.

"Hush, Jenny," Mama said. "You get back to your house, and Lou, you come into the kitchen and start breakfast. I'll see what I can do when Mr. Rouse comes home."

I heard them coming up the steps, so I ran back through the breezeway into the house and to my room. I sat down on the edge of my bed and looked over at my dresser to my beloved Pinky Ann, a rag doll and secret companion, to whom I talked when no one was listening. Reaching over and picking up the doll, I placed her on the bed and asked her what to do. "Pinky," I said, "which one would you take to be your own true friend: Mama, Papa, Mammy, or Jenny?" Without blinking an eye, Pinky said, "Why, Papa, of course."

I burst out crying. Dear, dear Papa. Like Pinky, I, too, loved him beyond words. Papa had heard many of my conversations with the rag doll, but he never revealed a confidence. This time, however, I knew that I should not breathe a word. Human events beyond my comprehension were taking place; yet I understood something of what was going on. Life had presented me with my first problem. How to solve it I couldn't imagine.

Instinctively I knew that something had happened between Jenny and Bill, something that belonged outside the world of my childhood. Because Jenny had told me not to tell anyone about what I had witnessed between her and Bill, I was cut off from my only source of information—Papa.

That evening, as we sat on the front porch, Papa with his pipe, Mama with her sewing, and I with Pinky Ann beside me, I thought of Jenny. "Mama," I asked, "is Mammy really going to whup Jenny?"

"In the first place, Catherine," Mama replied, "don't use the word 'whup.' The word is 'whip'."

"I know," I answered. "But Mammy said she was going to 'whup' Jenny; and since she is going to do the 'whupping,' why can't she call it 'whup'?"

"Because Mammy says 'whup' doesn't make it the right word to use," Mama snapped.

Papa had taken the pipe from his mouth and was watching us. "What about Jenny being whipped?" he asked.

"Papa!" I cried, jumping up and running to him. "Mammy said Jenny is going to have a baby. She made Jenny cry and said she was going to whup the life out of her if she didn't tell her his name. What did Mammy mean, Papa?"

Papa sat there a few minutes, not saying anything. Then finally, with a sigh, he got up. Putting me aside, he turned to Mama. "I'm going to Lou's and see what this is all about. I won't be long."

He left the porch, and Mama, Pinky Ann, and I remained in the fading twilight. The first stars began to appear, and just a thin slice of the moon moved up the sky from behind the house. Soon the evening was clamorous with a host of night insects. Across a patch of forest, I could hear the faint plaintive notes of the whippoorwill.

It was always a lonely time for me, the first part of twilight. Now, for comfort, I crept toward Mama and crawled into her lap. She had stopped sewing and sat with her hands crossed over my shoulders. I began to cry.

"No, baby," she said, squeezing me gently. "Jenny is in a little trouble, but it's nothing to kill anyone for."

"What kind of trouble, Mama?"

"When you're older, you'll understand. You're too young

to worry your head now with such thoughts." She sat, silently thinking for a moment. Then she said, "Why don't you take Pinky Ann and get ready for bed? I'll come up in a minute and hear your prayers and tuck you in. If Daddy comes home soon, he'll come up and kiss you good night. Now, go along."

Mama had turned on her sweetest smile; and when she did that, I willingly went into the house. I always wanted to please Mama.

It was not long after I had climbed into bed that I heard Papa's voice. Then he tiptoed into my room. I pretended to be asleep and waited for his lips to press my cheek. But he did not kiss me. He stood close to my bed, not moving. When I finally dared to open my eyes, the room was empty.

I must have slept that night because the next thing I knew daylight was streaming into my room through the open window. A new day had begun for me.

I didn't want any breakfast; not that I was sick, I just wasn't hungry. Papa fussed over me a bit, kissing my forehead and asking me if I felt all right. I wanted to go down to Jenny's house to see how she was, but I knew better than to ask.

Downstairs, I peeked into the kitchen, watching Mammy throw the pots and pans onto the stove, muttering to herself. The kitchen was no place for me, so I eased out into the side yard. After hesitating a few minutes, I paced the entire length of the picket fence, running my fingers over each point as I went. When I reached the gate, I pushed it open and sauntered into the apple orchard. I looked back at the house for an instant; then suddenly, I raced all the way through the apple trees and climbed the rail fence separating the orchard from the wheat field. I ran through the wheat, at this time of year up to my shoulders, and came to the road beyond the field, a narrow dirt road that led to Mammy's house.

Until now I had not been afraid; but the silence of this part of the farm began to creep in on me, and I found myself darting frightened glances into the woods bordering the road.

At last I reached the end of the lane. I could see the cabin where Mammy lived, made of logs and with tiny porches at the front and back. From the chimney, a thin spiral of blue smoke streamed straight up into the clear sky. Wild roses grew on the broken fence surrounding the yard, which had no grass, the ground being hard and dry under the trees.

The door of the cabin had no screen and flies buzzed in and out. A chicken ran cackling from behind an old bench as I approached the porch. On tiptoe, I looked inside. Still there were no signs of Jenny or her brothers and sisters about. I started to enter, but the acid stench of stale urine, together with the strong smell of cabbage cooking on the small stove, drove me back to the porch. "Jenny," I cried out. "Jenny, where are you?"

Then I heard the scuffle of bare feet coming out of the room to the right of the door. And there was Jenny. She stared at me from swollen eyes. She looked so sick. Suddenly I wanted to cry, sad at the sight of my friend living in such a squalid, dirty room, seeing her so ill and unhappy. I ran to her and pressed my head against her legs. I had never known a sad, sick, bad-smelling Jenny. She had always been clean and fresh and smiling at my house. I couldn't believe this was my Jenny. "What's the matter, Jenny?" I sobbed.

She just held me tighter.

"Tell me and I'll tell Papa. He'll make everything all right."

Jenny stiffened.

"You'll tell me, won't you, Jenny?"

"Hush now 'n' git outta here. Here comes ole Mr. Jones and he's lookin' mean. You just git outen the way and run fast 'n' quick all the way back to your house, y'hear?"

I ran through the house and out the back door. I started across the yard, then stopped. I'm not going home, I told myself, and I crept back to the porch. I crouched down close to the door and listened.

Tom Jones, Bill's father, worked for Papa. I used to see

him around the barn, but I didn't know he visited Jenny. Now I was full of curiosity. I peeped through the half–open door.

Jenny was leaning her weight against the front door, try-ing to hold it shut, while Mr. Jones pushed from the outside. "Let me in, Jenny gal," he called. "I ain't gonna hurt you."

"You go 'way, go clear 'way from this place," Jenny said.

"Let me in now, gal."

"Go 'way. You no good, Mistah Tom." Jenny was crying now, still trying to hold the door.

"Open up, Jenny. Iffen you don't, I'm gonna beat you when I get in. And you know I always get what I come after." He laughed now.

"Please, Mistah Tom!"

Finally, being stronger than Jenny, he pushed the door open. Chasing her, he caught her by the arm and slapped her face. "Take that, you black bitch!"

Jenny fell to the floor. "Don't, Mistah Tom, don't!" she cried, hiding her head in her arms.

"Git up, gal. I ain't gonna hurt you, not if you tell the truth."

"I done tole you the truth, Mistah Tom." Jenny cowered in a ball on the floor.

"You been playin' around with my boy Bill, ain't ya?"

Jenny cried harder, her back rising and falling with each sob. "Yes, sir . . . it's him."

Mr. Jones began to laugh. But it was different from ordi-nary laughter—like something I had never heard. I pulled the crack of the door farther open to see Mr. Jones bent over Jenny now, pulling off her ragged dress. I felt a shiver go through me.

Jenny was naked. She was black and her stomach was sticking out. She was holding one hand over her breasts and the other between her legs. Mr. Jones slapped her again and again, first on her cheeks, then on her bottom. Jenny lay crouched on the floor. "Please! Please!" she pleaded.

I did not stop to think. I only knew that this man, Tom Jones, was hurting Jenny. I ran into the cabin, screaming, and began kicking at him. He turned, surprised and angry. "Why, you little sneak," he snapped, grabbing me by my long hair. "I ought to kill you here and now."

I sank my teeth into his lower leg, and he let go with a curse. I turned and scrambled through the open door and made it to the road. I ran until I could run no more. When I reached the wheat field, I lay down and tried to hold my breath, fearing he might find me as he thrashed around in the field, looking, calling, "I know yer in there. Now, come on out!" But he did not find me.

I don't know how long I lay there before I heard Mammy coming down the road. She was talking to herself. "Wunda wher that po' chile be?"

I jumped up and ran onto the road, crying to her.

"Lordy, bless my soul, Li'l Missy, whar you bin? They's lookin', callin' for you. Yo' daddy done tore his hair out. He's like a wile man."

I cried until Mammy picked me up and stepped off the road and under a tree. Sitting down, she took me in her lap and began to rock and sing. I must have fallen asleep.

I awoke in my own bed at home. Papa was sitting in a chair beside me. Before opening my eyes, I heard Papa tell Mama that Jenny had told him the whole story.

"What did you do?" Mama asked.

"Took my gun and went to the Jones house and fired him."

"Did he behave badly?"

"Well," Papa began, "he started talking about his contract for a year's work. But when I told him what Jenny had told me . . . well, that seemed to take the tar out of him."

"Then what did he do?"

"I told him to be gone by daylight, and I sat on my horse until I saw him go toward his shed for his mule and wagon. I guess he's gone by now."

"Let's hope so," Mama said.

"But, to be sure, I'm going to ride over there and see," Papa answered, "just as soon as Cathy wakes."

With that, I rolled over and sat up in bed.

"Here's our girl," Papa said.

I put my arms around his neck, pulling him close to me.

"Now, you just jump up and eat a good breakfast."

"And," Mama said, "guess who's out in the kitchen laughing and waiting for you."

"Jenny?" I questioned.

"None other."

After dressing, I raced to the kitchen and there, sure enough, were Jenny and Mammy, laughing and talking together as if yesterday had never been.

But it had been. And because of it, I was never to be the same little girl again. I knew now what it meant to have a baby. I knew the meaning of heartache, misery, and tears. But most of all, I knew that people would never be to me what they once were—not men, anyway. They would not all be knights on white chargers. And maybe Papa would never be again, either. That was the real heartbreak. Men were men. Papa was a man. My bewilderment, heartbreak, and suspicion stayed with me into maturity.

3

A Time to Grow

PAPA'S EFFORTS HAD BROUGHT ABOUT adequate roads, mail delivery, and later telephones; but there were still very few schools in the area, so he set about to find a teacher who would live with us and teach me. He finally located a Miss McKinley, from Massachusetts, who had retired as a teacher because of her health and who was willing to share our lovely farm and instruct me until I was old enough to go to a boarding school.

She arrived one fine fall day, and the next I saw of her was in an upstairs bedroom with maps, charts, and blackboards all lined up and a special desk and chair for me. I felt very important, dressed in a starched and fluffy dress. I had no idea what school was, but I was excited and happy at the prospect.

The procedure was two hours of spelling and writing with Miss McKinley and one hour of piano with Aunt Cora, my father's old maid sister who lived with Grandmother Rouse. After dinner there were two more hours of mathematics and geography before my classwork ended with Miss McKinley reading a book to me.

Life was wonderful. The summer days were filled with swimming, drinking lemonade in the shade of the huge oaks in the front yard, fishing with my father as we sat on a cool creek bank, or riding with him on my own horse over the farm in the late afternoons. The evening brought fried chicken suppers, moonlight, and the smell of flowers blooming under the bedroom windows.

I was an active little girl, riding, studying, and observing all that went on around me. I knew as much about the work at the barns and the distillery as I did about the affairs around the house. Every morning my father would get on his horse and go to the distillery to see if all was well there. Then he would ride over the farm checking on things until dinner time.

At 11:30 a big bell that hung on the back porch would be rung, and the men would come in with the teams. After watering the mules and the horses, they would eat a big dinner, then lie down in the shade of a tree for a half hour's nap before returning to the fields. By then both men and animals were rested and ready for six or seven more hours of work in the afternoon. This was at the peak of the season of putting in the crops. The fall and winter work was lighter, with repairing of fences and barns. Harness mending was done in a barn on cold afternoons, when man and beast wanted to be inside.

It was a quiet, peaceful, secure, and happy way of living. We made our own amusements, such as reading aloud in the evening after supper, or Mama's playing the piano while Papa's baritone voice joined her more timid soprano in singing the simple tunes she played. Sometimes someone in the neighborhood would give a dance, and they would mount their horses— Mama always riding side-saddle—and off they would go for an evening of fun, leaving me at home with Miss McKinley or with Mammy when Miss McKinley wanted to join them.

I was Papa's constant companion. He taught me to swim like an eel, ride like a fiend, and have a horror of telling a lie. He used to say, "Cath, I can't teach you how to be a lady, but I can teach you how to behave like a gentleman."

I remember one warm May day when Miss McKinley had declared a half holiday because the spring fever had me drooping over my books. She suggested I go for a ride to clear my head, and I jumped at the idea. Rushing to the barn, I saddled my horse, Nell, and was gone in a matter of minutes into the meadows, sweet with wild grass from which flocks of birds rose as I galloped along. On the ride back I had to cross a small creek, usually very shallow, to reach the road to the barn. When I got there, Nell pulled up to take a well–deserved drink of the water running pure and cold over the rocks of the creek bed. Something alerted her, and she lifted her head from the water and stood as though listening. Just then I heard a roar and turned to see a wall of yellow water almost on me. As the flash flood hit, I heard my father yell from the bank, "Hold on to her mane, baby, Nell will bring you out!"

The water struck with such force that Nell was knocked off her feet, but she came up swimming with me clinging to her mane. I still shudder at the memory of that terror. Trees were rushing past; but Nell, like the white charger in my old storybook, swam with her head held high with me clinging to her like a drowning puppy. I remember the tiredness of my arms and the panic of those moments in the water—it seemed as if time had stopped. Then I heard my father laugh: "You're all right, baby. Just hold on a little longer. Old Nell is almost out of the water. You should see what a picture you and Nell make! Wish I had a picture machine so you could see it later." This was Papa's way of keeping up my courage—and it worked.

Time raced on, and I was reaching young womanhood. When I was thirteen years old, the big decision was made to send Miss McKinley back to Boston—and to send me to boarding school.

I overheard Papa explaining to Mama that the time had come for me to be sent away to school "to sorta tame her down." He favored the convent that was close by, but Mama didn't want me to go to the convent because I might become a Catholic.

"Damn, Nance, if you don't get the craziest ideas! What harm will being a Catholic do her? She's nothing now anyway."

I wept alone in my room. I didn't know what it meant to be nothing. I didn't want to go to the convent. I didn't want to be a Catholic. What was a Catholic anyway? As the day grew close when I would leave home for life in the convent school, I went around with downcast eyes, looking so mournful that my father called me before him.

"Papa," I sobbed, "I don't want to go."

"Well, you are going, and that's a fact. So don't whine about it. Gentlemen don't cry, you know."

"But," I protested, "I'm not a gentleman. I'm only a girl."

Though I wept and moaned, preparations went steadily ahead for my entering Nazareth Academy in September 1913.

One morning I was awakened by the firm, quick step of my father coming up the stairs. I sat up in bed expectantly, awaiting his arrival; but even as I heard the door opening I remembered that this was the day that I was to leave home. At once I was seized with pangs of anguish, which I later identified as homesickness. But never having had a reason to be homesick before, I didn't know what was the matter with me.

Entering the door, Papa said, "Come, daughter, get up and be quick about it. We are leaving within the hour."

I looked at him. "No cream toddy?" I questioned.

"No," he replied. "No more cream toddies . . . no more babying. You begin your adult life today, and damn if it isn't hard on all of us." He took a freshly laundered handkerchief from his trouser pocket and blew his nose. I knew I shouldn't cry. Papa hated tears in grown people, but I couldn't hold back the tears.

I remember crying over and over, "Don't make me go away. Please don't make me leave." Yet, within the hour, I was in the car with Beau-Pup, my beloved dog, who had succeeded Pinky Ann as my faithful friend, clutched firmly in my arms. I had made up my mind that if I had to go, at least my dog was going too.

Mama, looking very pretty, cool, and collected, was in front with Papa. She had a veil over her leghorn hat and she sat quite still. Papa, his driving cap pulled low over his brow, tried to start the car with all the usual ceremony. But dignity was soon forgotten. Those automobiles of 1913 were death to dignity. I sat in the back with Beau and didn't laugh as Papa had his usual trouble getting the car started. Mama was always expected to pull down the spark while Papa turned the crank; but she was never quick enough, and the engine would die. Papa finally gave up asking her. After turning the crank, he would race to the spark on the steering wheel of the car. He rarely made it the first time; but after three or four false starts, he would reach the spark in time to keep the engine going. I usually giggled throughout the performance, and Papa would get mad and shout, "Stop that silly laughter." But this morning I didn't laugh and he didn't shout. In fact, he grinned when the car died, and he kept looking at me, trying to get me to laugh.

That day I had no heart for laughter. I said a silent good-bye to the trees in the yard I'd sat under so many times on long summer afternoons, dreaming my dreams of faraway places. As we crossed the creek, I wished I were that creek so that I could always be in the same place—not thinking that the water in the creek was moving along to its rendezvous with the sea. As I saw Nell grazing in the meadow, I wished that I were she and could stay on the farm forever. My heart was bursting with loneliness as I said good-bye to all the dear and familiar scenes of my childhood.

We arrived at Nazareth at eleven that morning and were taken on a tour of the convent farm and the convent itself. Beau-Pup ran along, merrily barking at everything that he saw, and I, watching him, wished that I were Beau-Pup. All that day I wished that I were something other than myself . . . the car, Mama, Papa, anything to get out of leaving my home to come to this school.

After our tour, we were introduced to Mother Rose, director general of the motherhouse that headed all of the Sisters of Charity of Nazareth hospitals and schools throughout the United States. And while we were talking—at least Mama and Papa were talking; I was so scared I never opened my mouth—in bustled another nun, and I was told she would have direct control of my days in the convent. To me, who had never seen a nun before, these good women were the most terrifying sights I had ever beheld. Being country-bred, I naturally compared them to the animals with which I was familiar. Sister Illuminata looked like a fox, her bright eyes shining in her little heart-shaped face, her figure concealed under the rusty black habit of her order, giving the impression of bulk and power. She was truly a frightening person. As she took my arm, she told me she would be my wardrobe mistress and recreation director for the time that I was to be at Nazareth. I gave up all thoughts of ever being a free human being again. The years appeared to stretch ahead of me with no break in sight. I was to be a prisoner, cut off from the life that had been such a pleasure to me.

I was allowed to have lunch with Mama and Papa in the guest dining room, and then the hour of parting came. I stood in the parlor watching Mama and Papa preparing to leave, holding Beau so tight he nearly strangled.

Mother Rose, the gentlest of women, murmured that I would be in good hands, and she shook hands with my parents. She gave me the sweetest smile, which sealed me to her forever. For the next few years, I was to solve many problems at her knees, never doubting her love and always sure that her wise counsel would be for my benefit.

As they were about to leave, Papa called me to him. "Goodbye, honey," he said. "Remember all that I have told you and let the Sisters guide you for a while. They know what's best and will be glad to help you in the growing up that you have to do on your own."

I looked around wildly. There was no help from anyone. Mama stood looking out the window, and Beau whimpered. I sat down on a chair covered with horsehair and buried my face in the warm coat of Beau's back. My father had taught me to be ashamed to cry, but tears flowed anyway. I sat weeping with desolation and loneliness. Then the final blow fell. Sister Illuminata took Beau from my arms.

"Look, dear," she said kindly, "you can't keep your dog here. He must return with your parents."

I struggled to my feet and gave Beau to her, then, without looking at anyone, walked out of the parlor and started down the long corridor that led to the part of the convent where the school was. At that moment I did not realize it, but I was walking from babyhood into the life of a convent girl.

That night, when we retired for the evening, I found that convent girls slept in dormitories. I, as an only child, was used to the privacy of my own room, and now here I was in a vast room with row upon row of other girls. The lack of privacy was a frightening thing for me and I slept very little.

The next morning, as I washed in the common room with fifty or sixty other girls, I wondered what was wrong with me. Everyone else seemed so happy and gay and carefree, but I couldn't share their feelings. It was then that I resolved to kill myself. But how? That was the question.

The manner in which this could be done came to me that afternoon. I saw some apple trees, and on the trees, green apples. I remembered Mammy's dire predictions that green apples would kill a person if she ate enough of them. When someone died unexpectedly in the neighborhood, she always said, "I spec' they been eatin' green apples." I quickly gathered enough to fill the ample pockets of my uniform, and after lights were out I ate every one of them, cores and all.

It must have been midnight when the pain struck. I awakened with the most horrible cramps. "This is it," I thought. "This is death."

For the first half hour I bore the pain, but finally the vomiting began. I could no longer keep quiet. I heaved and moaned. I was so ill I could not make it to the washroom, and finally the noise of my illness must have reached Sister Illuminata. Through the waves of nausea I saw the gleam of a light and heard her irritated voice.

"What on earth is the matter with you, child?" she grumbled. But upon seeing the vomit and my apple-green complexion, she became concerned and hustled me off to the infirmary. I was nauseated for hours, but finally my stomach was emptied and I fell into an exhausted sleep.

When I awakened, it was late in the morning and my father was standing beside my bed. That morning we had our first long and serious talk. He was the only one who knew that I had eaten the apples with the intention of doing away with myself, and he at long last made me understand that one cannot run away from life. I became aware of many things, none of which I completely understood; but from then on I never again whimpered or tried to escape the changing fortunes of my life.

That first year in the convent was filled with study and exercise: fencing, dancing, walking. How I hated those afternoon walks. It might rain, snow, sleet, anything, but nothing daunted Sister Illuminata from getting us into our heavy coats and hoods and out for a mile-long afternoon walk every day but Sunday. We got out of it on Sunday, that is, *if* our parents came for a visit. Few showed up on those inclement Sundays, so walk we did, two by two, marching briskly down the long avenue until we reached the halfway mark. Then it was back to the convent, led by that indomitable, fanatically exercise-minded nun, who believed that an apple a day and a mile walk a day made a girl healthy and wise. She always left out the word "wealthy" for fear it would conjure up the idea of a future husband. She didn't want her girls to think of men.

We were not even allowed to hold hands or link our arms, and there was very little conversation as we walked; but when we turned around and headed for home, we quickened our pace, like horses heading back to the barn. The walks began in September and continued until May, with the exception of Christmas and Easter. Years later, when I saw films of Hitler's storm troopers, I remembered my marching days at Nazareth.

Our walks must have been a sight to see because in the spring five or six boys who lived in Bardstown would come to Nazareth in a car to watch the daily parade. One of the young men, Sam Conner, would often throw me a box of candy. Of course, the girls would grab for the candy and Sister would try to take it away.

I met Sam my first winter at school, when I was thirteen years old. We had a heavy snow one night, and the nuns gave us a sleigh ride. We were all having a wonderful time and were particularly excited because, when we got to Bardstown, we were to go to Lawson's, a soda fountain, and have a chocolate drink.

When we got there, everybody stood up and got out of the sleigh but me. I stood up and fell into the worst snowbank imaginable. I was buried. Sam was one of the boys who had been standing around watching all of this, and he came and dug me out. He told me later it was at that moment he decided he would marry me one day.

One afternoon when we girls set out for a long snowy walk, I edged up to Sister Illuminata and asked her if I might walk with her so in case she slipped in the snow I would be there to help her. Sister, who was very wise in her judgment of the girls, glanced at me suspiciously out of her bright, keen eyes. "Yes, of course," she said, "but why, after all these months, have you become so solicitous of my welfare?"

Sister was right. I did have an ulterior motive. A few days earlier, I had seen a smiling face as my group of freshmen passed a group of seniors. (Different classes were not allowed to walk together.) This senior was beautiful—curly brown hair, shining blue eyes, a peach and apple complexion, and a slim little body. I made up my mind that I wanted to make a special friend.

In those days we called such attachments "Love Bests." It was innocent, exciting, but frowned on by the Sisters—why, I couldn't imagine.

On this snowy day, as I walked beside Sister conjuring up the courage to ask her for permission for an introduction to the senior girl, the wind was blowing hard and Sister was having trouble with her long black veil, which was almost whipped off her head by a particularly vicious swipe of the wind. I grabbed the veil and held onto it while Sister tried to hold her cape. Finally we conquered both.

Sister grabbed her whistle and blew one long blast. "Back . . . back to school. The weather is too severe." She wheeled in her tracks, and we all started running toward the convent. The snow, hail, and wind were turning into a bad storm. As we ran, sure enough, Sister's feet slipped out from under her and down she went . . . ker-plopp. We all rushed to get her up, but her dignity had been upset. She was so cross that I dared not present the request I had intended.

After we had hot chocolate and warmed ourselves at the radiators, Sister came grumbling up to me. "What did you want, Catherine, when you offered to accompany me on our"—she grinned, showing she did have a sense of humor— "ill-fated walk? I know you had some reason. Didn't you?"

"Yes, Sister," I replied. "I wanted permission to talk to a senior by the name of Duane. I liked her and she seemed to be so friendly."

Sister looked at the floor for a few minutes, then she

shuffled off, muttering, "I'll see what can be done." In a few days she introduced me to Dorothy and her mother.

On the Saturday I first met Dorothy, we became fast friends and I was introduced to one of the most delightful families I've ever known. I spent many summer weeks at the Duane home in Louisville.

4

The Picnic

WHEN AMERICA ENTERED WORLD WAR I in 1917, Sam Conner joined the aviation branch of the army, which was in its infancy. Oh, my, he was so handsome in his uniform, I fell in love with him. I had been a little bit in love with him ever since he'd dug me out of the snowbank.

It seemed as though every time Sam came home from the army to visit, we would have a big storm and the creek on our farm would rise. Sam wouldn't be able to get across so my father would take me to meet him by the creek bank. Sam would holler over, "How are you?"

I couldn't yell loud enough so my father would answer for me: "She's doing pretty well."

Thus the conversation would go, back and forth. You can imagine how satisfactory it was. Sam was stationed at the base in Dayton, Ohio, and I saw him only occasionally.

And then 1920 came along. I had graduated from Nazareth's high school, attended a junior college for two years in Lexington, and spent one year at the University of Louisville. Everyone would say, "Oh, you don't want to work; why keep on going to school and getting degrees?" And Sam kept asking me to marry him. So I did.

My father wanted to give me some sort of wedding gift. He always believed in giving money or land. Though he was not wealthy, he had been a conservative man and had enough money to buy me a house.

One cold winter night in 1921, Will Stiles of Bardstown came to ask my father to join him in purchasing Federal Hill (the estate that was to become My Old Kentucky Home). Mr. Stiles explained that Mrs. Frost, then the owner, needed money and was willing to sell the property for $65,000. If the needed improvements were made, Will believed it could become a tourist attraction.

My father was interested. He thought it might be both a home for me and a source of revenue. It would be hard work for me to care for such a place, but Papa felt I would have an adequate income for life if it became a tourist attraction.

We drove out to Federal Hill and found it a complete wreck. Shutters were hanging awry, windowpanes were broken, doors that would not shut were hanging from their hinges, weeds and brush reached up to the very steps leading into the main part of the house. Snakes were crawling everywhere, and wasps hung from a large nest over the front door. It was a sight! There was nothing there but ruins, hardly a vestige of what had been a beautiful plantation. Looking around, Papa said, "This is what happens when the money runs out."

Mrs. Frost was gracious. She received us in the main hall, where old sheets and remnants of bedspreads were draped over doors and windows to keep the heat in on cold days. She admitted that her money had run out and so she offered to sell her house and acreage for $65,000.

Well, $65,000 for a rundown plantation—acres of land uncultivated for many years, outbuildings in total disrepair, and a house in unbelievable ruin—was a stiff price in 1921. If Stephen Foster had not visited there and received his inspiration to write "My Old Kentucky Home," the property would have been worth about $10,000, if that much. The postwar boom had not yet reached small-town Kentucky. Times were hard, land was cheap, and Bardstown was the small seat of a poor county with little of any importance except that it had the first cathedral west of the Alleghenies.

Having been brought up to be loyal to and protective of one's home environment, I talked to my father after we left Federal Hill. "Papa," I said, "I don't want that place. I'll be dead before I can restore it, even if I do take in tourists. Why don't we see if the state of Kentucky can take it over?" When we reached home, we called politicians J. Dan Talbott and Arch Pullium, banker Henry Muir, lawyer Ernest Fulton, and a few other Bardstown residents for a consultation.

Dan Talbott and my father saw the possibilities for a great tourist attraction. But the governor, Edwin Morrow, was a Republican, and Dan, Papa, and most of us gathered that evening were Democrats. Dan's political intuition kicked in. "Let's call Osso Stanley," he said. "He's very close to Governor Morrow."

We called Stanley, a Republican lawyer in Bardstown, who, after listening closely, agreed that Federal Hill should become a state park. I suggested that we go as a group to Frankfort to see the governor. Among those who went were Stanley, Talbott, Pullium, Fulton, Will Stiles, and my father. Governor Morrow was interested, but, to our great disappointment, he explained that there was no money in the treasury for a state park.

The evening after our return to Bardstown, we met in Ernest Fulton's office. In addition to those who had gone to Frankfort, banker Lewis Guthrie, his wife, Amy, and I were present. We decided to solicit the people of Bardstown for funds, especially those whose businesses might profit from tourist trade. There were a few restaurants, two hotels, and two drugstores. Little money was collected, and people throughout the state weren't particularly interested in establishing a park in Bardstown, especially because there was much doubt cast on the story that Foster actually had written "My Old Kentucky Home" while visiting there.

Mrs. Guthrie and I went out again to visit Mrs. Frost. She insisted that Foster had written his plaintive and sentimental melody at a particular desk. She pointed it out, still sitting in the hallway. We believed her, so the next day Amy and I drove to Louisville to visit her friend, Mrs. Millard Cox. We told our story and asked for her opinion. She made a suggestion that had been in my mind: "How about letting the children of Kentucky contribute to the project?"

We thought it was a fine idea, and Mrs. Cox offered to have cardboard replicas made of the house at Federal Hill with a hole in the chimney through which pennies could be dropped. Mrs. Guthrie and I drove miles and miles visiting schoolrooms all over Kentucky. The schoolchildren contributed some $45,000. Judge Robert Worth Bingham of Louisville, owner of the *Courier-Journal,* offered $5,000, and Mrs. Frost agreed to sell the property for $50,000.

When the house was dedicated and its name changed to My Old Kentucky Home, Governor Morrow said, "This song has touched the heart of the world. It comes from the pennies of childhood. It comes from the poor in purse but rich in heart."

In March 1921, my son was born. Never had I seen such a beautiful baby. He had reddish blond hair, bright blue eyes, rosy cheeks, and a ready smile on his chubby face. To me he was the one perfect person in my life. In the beginning, there had been Mama and Papa, and now I had my beloved Jimmy, who was named after my father.

Not long after Jimmy was born, I found out that my husband, Sam, had overextended himself in his hardware business and was on the way to losing it. I spoke to my father, who at once looked into the finances of the store and found that it was indeed about to go into bankruptcy. He came to the conclusion that $100,000 might see the company through. The banks refused the company's request for a loan of that amount. In 1921 that was considered a lot of money for a small hardware firm in a little country town. After studying the matter closely, my father lent us the money.

When the transaction had been completed, Papa had a long business talk with me. He told me Sam needed help badly, and he believed I was the one to give it to him. I was startled. I knew nothing about business. But Papa went on to explain that our hardware company dealt in cement, dynamite, and building materials, and he believed Kentucky was going to build cement roads. He told me he knew many contractors and had a friend who served as chairman of the State Highway Commission. His plan was for me to appear at the "lettings," the meetings in Frankfort, the state capital, to award the contracts to the lowest bidder for sections of road, bridges, everything concerned with highway construction. Papa showed me how to make bids on certain sections. My mission was to sell the cement and dynamite for the road building.

I was frightened at the idea of entering this exclusively male field, but I felt it was my duty. I had not yet had a taste of the excitement of competition. It wasn't long before I found myself seated in the office of the chairman of the State Highway Commission, with half a dozen men, most of them smoking and shuffling papers at the other end of the table from me and giving me speculative stares. When the commissioners came in, the chairman, J.C.W. Beckham, a tall, white-haired former U.S. congressman, addressed us.

"Gentlemen and Mrs. Conner," he said, "this is a most auspicious occasion. Today we are going to begin a long-range road-building program, starting with a trial run of ten miles of concrete for testing purposes. This is to be an entirely new conception of road building in Kentucky. Our dirt and gravel will not stand up to the traffic we hope to attract to our state. Our economy needs bolstering, and this administration intends to go after not only industry but the tourist trade that will be attracted by good roads. Well, gentlemen?"

He leaned back in his chair and closed his eyes.

The men were on their feet, waving their cigars, cigarettes, and pipes, each trying to get the eye of the chairman—now I realized why he'd closed his eyes. "Order, order!" he thundered. "One at a time, please, each of you pass up your bids, and in due time you will be notified what company turned in the most acceptable bid."

Confusion reigned. None of the men had come prepared to submit a written bid. Only I had. My father had drawn it up, and I passed it to the chairman. "Thank you, Mrs. Conner," he said. "It will be a pleasure doing business with someone so well versed in the etiquette of letting bids."

As I was leaving the capitol, I stopped, despite a cold breeze, to enjoy the view from the steps. The sun was setting, and the great, golden ball sent out shafts that lighted the dome of the capitol and flashed off the windows of buildings, turning the drab little town into a dazzle of lights. As I started down the steps again, I heard someone call my name. Turning, I saw Bill Devereaux, one of my competitors, who was also active in politics. Politely, I asked him what he wanted.

"What do I want? I want to know how you got into this game and how you knew to submit your bid in writing." He hesitated. "We've never done that before."

I giggled, naively. "A little bird told me."

"I'm wondering if the Old Eagle might be that bird."

"Old Eagle?" I asked, honestly puzzled.

"You don't know who the Old Eagle is?" he asked. "It's the chairman, the Old Eagle who swoops down on lovely ladies like yourself and carries them off to his nest high in the hotel." He grinned. Then he asked me to have dinner with him because he was going to have to stay over to write up his bid. Disgusted and furious, I declined, saying I had to return home.

"You're pretty green, aren't you?" He smiled smugly. "Don't you know I can throw you enough business to make you the greatest salesman—or saleswoman—in this state if you play it wise, or I can fix it so you won't get one bit of business, now or ever?"

I drove home deeply disturbed, realizing what I was up against if I expected to be a success in this men's world. My first venture into the business world showed me what my life was to be. But succeed I did, and, after some ten years, Sam was able to pay off his indebtedness.

To keep me busy I had my business selling cement and dynamite, a beautiful little boy, and a nice home with a jewel of a cook. What more could a woman want, I wondered. The years passed quickly, pleasantly, and uneventfully, until one morning in 1928.

J. Dan Talbott, famed in Kentucky politics as a "Champion of Good Government," was a man who, for more than a quarter of a century, had from behind the scenes directed much of the action of Democratic political leaders in Kentucky. He was a neighbor and a friend of mine, and it was through him that I had my first encounter with politics.

One morning, answering a knock on my door, I opened it to find a smiling Mr. Talbott standing on my doorstep. Behind him lurked two other men, peering at me over their wire-rimmed glasses.

Dan greeted me with a strange remark: "Well, I bring you your future. Catherine," he said, "this is Captain Cardin, and of course you know Ernest Fulton." Fulton, a prominent lawyer in town, was a close friend of my father's and mine.

"How do you do, gentlemen," I said by way of a greeting. "What brings you to my house this early in the morning?"

"These men are soliciting votes, money, help, and what have you in their effort to capture for Captain Cardin the nomination for Congress from the Fourth District," Dan replied. "Bill Devereaux suggested we come to you."

I stared at them. "You want me to help? Because whatever you want, Dan, I will try to do it for you."

Mr. Cardin interrupted. "Mrs. Conner, we want young people to get interested in the government, and I believe the way to do it is to get them involved in politics. I have been told that you know a great many people and that you are very persuasive when you speak. Your precinct has always gone Republican because of the black population. Have you any idea how we Democrats might carry it?"

"What makes you think I might know how to do the impossible?" I asked.

"Well," he countered, "you can sell cement, dynamite, and lumber. Surely you can sell your party."

"Heavens!" I replied. "You have posed a real problem. But let me think and maybe I'll come up with some ideas."

Mr. Cardin looked at me long and hard. "I believe you will," he said. They left and I settled down to think through this new challenge.

A few hours later, I heard my father rushing up onto the porch. Bursting in, he said, "Catherine, did you know that Dan Talbott and Captain Cardin have suggested your name to the local committee for precinct chairman?"

"But you and Dan know that I don't know a thing about politics. They didn't accept me, did they?" I asked.

"Yes," replied my father. "That's why I came hurrying out here. I want to know what you think about it."

"Oh, Lordy," I moaned. "You know I am under obligation to Dan. If he wants me to do it, I will. But how on earth am I to think of a way for the Democrats to carry a precinct that has always been Republican? It just can't be done!"

I remember hesitating, Well, I was thinking, maybe there was a way.

My father looked at me with a quizzical smile. "Think, think, think," he said. "And again I say *think*. That's all you have to do. From somewhere, you will find the answer." He left the house and hurried to his car. I knew he was going to tell the committee I would take the job.

Later that night I called Dan. "Isn't Al Smith running for president in this election?" I asked.

"Yes," he said, "and that won't make your job any easier. But I know how resourceful and energetic you are, Catherine. Just keep in touch with me, and if you have any ideas, call me. After all, you women have gotten the right to vote, and that carries with it the responsibility not only of voting but also working at the polls. You women may live to regret having to shoulder such responsibilities, but they are yours."

"Yes," I sighed. "I'm living to regret it already. In some telephone conversations I've had lately, a lot of people say the pope will be brought over here to live and rule if a Catholic like Al Smith wins the election."

"You are so right," said Dan, and he hung up.

Late that night I had the idea. Why don't I give my cook Tilly a picnic? She hasn't had a day off since she began working for us. I'll let her ask her friends. We can have it at the fairgrounds. I'll furnish the beer, moonshine (legal whiskey wasn't returned to the United States until President Franklin D. Roosevelt's administration repealed the Volstead Act in 1933), and the food. It'll be a real wingding of a party.

I awakened my husband, Sam, to tell him about my notion. He agreed that this just might turn the tide in my precinct, but he cautioned me not to say a word about it until he looked into whether it would be feasible.

The next morning, Sam left for his hardware store and I broached the idea to Tilly. That precious black jewel gave a whoop of joy. "Lordy, Lordy, what a nice thing you are doing, Missy. I is pleased to death and I do accept. All my friends will, too. You can just bet on it." Tilly chuckled all day over the prospect, and dinner that night was not up to her usual standards. Clearly, she had other things on her mind.

Each morning that followed, she gave me a running account of who would be there. Pretty soon I suspected that the idea had caught on and the town's entire black population was coming to Tilly's picnic. Each night, Sam and I added more trucks for transporting her guests to the fairgrounds to the already impressive group of ten. I increased the food allotment, but the entertainment remained the same—a jug band, beer, and moonshine.

On the night of November 6, Tilly rushed into the living room in a great dither. "Oh, Missy, Missy," she cried, "all my friends been coming to see me all day. They's so worried. Did you know that tomorrow's election day?" She glanced at me with shining brown eyes from under lowered eyelids, in which I could see suspicion struggling with her desire to know that I was innocent of any wrongdoing. She struggled on. "All my friends say the 'Publicans gonna kill 'em if dey ain't here to vote tomorrow." She scratched her head. "I is all tuckered out with thinkin'." She sagged into a chair for support.

I jumped to my feet. "Oh, my, imagine our not thinking of that! What will we do? We have all the food—fried chicken, potato salad, steaks, hot dogs, beer, cider, moonshine, ice cream, cake—and music. Don't forget the music, Tilly. We just can't think of not having it, can we?" I asked the faithful soul standing there, a mass of misery.

"No'm, not after all that trouble," Tilly muttered.

"Oh," I ran to her, "I have it! I'll have the trucks pick you up before six in the morning and you can come home early— say, around four o'clock. Then everyone can vote and you'll have your picnic, too. OK?"

"Yes'm, that sound all right to me. I'll go tell them right now, if you don't mind," answered a thoroughly reassured Tilly.

Sam and I arose at four the next morning. We went to the warehouse and saw the eighteen trucks filled with food and drink pull out at five o'clock. We followed the trucks as they gathered up Tilly's friends, some 350 of them, and set off for the picnic grounds. Upon arrival, they saw the fires burning and smelled coffee and hotcakes cooking for their breakfast. Everybody seemed to be in a fine humor, and the picnic began with a bang. As we left the fairgrounds, we saw the stone jugs beginning to circulate.

The Picnic

The November air was nippy that election day, but the sun was warm. Scarlet and green leaves floated lazily to the ground, and the people responded to the weather. In town, the women with scarves tied around their heads were happy, going to the polls dressed in their bright election clothes. They wanted to gossip as well as vote. The records of the candidates did not mean much to them, but the voting place, where they met friends and neighbors, had great appeal. The different missionary societies were selling coffee and pies at the voting places, and farmers and their wives were coming into town for a holiday. They arrived in trucks and old cars and on foot. There was gaiety in the air, and everyone was in the same mood as the picnickers at the fairgrounds.

As I voted, I wondered how the real picnickers were doing. Catching Sam's eye across the crowd, I beckoned to him. When he was within earshot, I asked, "Have you heard anything?"

"Have I!" he grinned. "I just came from the fairgrounds, and they are having the time of their lives. The contests are on, and Hawk just won the potato race. He pushed that potato with his nose, and it didn't roll more than two inches from a true course at any time during the whole race."

"What was the prize for the race?" I asked.

"I think it was five dollars. Hawk would do anything for money, you know."

"Oh, how I know," I murmured. "Hawk" Rogers, known in Bardstown for serving the best food in town at his restaurant, worked for me on and off over the years.

"By the way," Sam said, looking at his watch, "the Republicans are already becoming anxious. It's three-thirty . . . look out for some action around four."

On the dot of four Dan Talbott waylaid me on the sidewalk outside the courthouse. "Katy, do you know what has happened to all the Negroes? There hasn't been one around, and Weller Barnes and the boys have gone looking for them.

You know, of course, that we Democrats are carrying all seven precincts. But when the black vote begins to come in, our majority will melt like a snowball in hell."

I looked at him in consternation, not wanting to give away the secret.

He pushed back the iron-gray hair from that brow that I found so handsome. "I wish they wouldn't show," he said, "but they'll be here at the last hour and knock our majorities into a cocked hat. Well, I'll see you later, after we count the votes." With that, he moved off into the crowd.

I looked after him. "My dear Dan," I thought, "you who are so smart and so good that you have no idea that on this day we may," I remember crossing my fingers, "beat the Republicans through a ruse. Not honorable, not good, but effective."

As I walked to the little park between the courthouse and the post office, Weller Barnes, one of the local Republican workers, came running. "Catherine," he called, "did you stage a picnic for your cook today?"

"Yes," I replied, "I did. But they were to be back early in order to vote and," looking at my watch, "it's now four-thirty. I can't imagine what has kept them."

"I can tell you," said Leilan Hubbard, another Republican, puffing up. "They are all out at the fairgrounds, drunk as loons. The trucks have broken down, two are out of gas, three with flat tires; in fact, not one of those trucks can run!" He continued disgustedly, "No one seems to know what happened. We're sending cars out to get them."

"How many cars?" I asked innocently.

"Oh, we can find only ten or twelve, but they're gone lickety-split out to get them."

I knew by counting that 100 to 150 blacks would not make it to the polls in time, and a wave of elation swept over me. I didn't go home. I stood on the sidewalk for a few minutes and then ran to my car and drove out to the fairgrounds.

Such a scene met my eyes! Leilan had not exaggerated. Four or five cars were standing idle while their drivers were trying to round up passengers. But the picnic guests were full of the joy of life, drunk on their moonshine, and they didn't want to leave. Some were dancing, some singing sweetly to the Stephen Foster tunes the band was playing. And two fights were going on, with bets being wagered as to the winner. Finally, after much talk and the passing of many dollar bills, they were put into the cars and sped away.

I looked at my watch—ten to five. I knew I had carried my town for Captain Cardin and Al Smith. Smith may not carry the state, I told myself, but he was safe in my precinct.

I drove slowly down the tree-shaded road from the picnic grounds. Behind me, men from the various garages in town worked feverishly to get the trucks ready to roll. But I knew they would never make it in time. Success was sweet.

5

The Democratic Convention

AFTER MY SUCCESSFUL PICNIC, I rose from precinct chairman, to county chairman over twenty-two precincts, to chairman of my seventeen-county district. The following year I was selected by a Democratic majority to be the Democratic national committeewoman from Kentucky. My political star was rising.

My election did not come easily. It was bitterly contested by Ben Johnson, former Democratic congressman for the Fourth District (my district). He had been congressman for many years and had built up a good-sized following, and he wanted his wife to hold the position of national committeewoman from Kentucky.

Much scandal was implied about me. John Y. Brown Sr., who was prompted by the Johnson faction, said in a speech in Bardstown that was broadcast on the radio that state senator Happy Chandler was singing love songs in front of the white-columned porch of my house in Bardstown while Dan Talbott was upstairs with me. It was enough to send my mother to the hospital and my father to the town square carrying a pistol, which he swore he would use if he met the son of a bitch who told those lies about my character. The going had been rough to win the office of Democratic national committeewoman from Kentucky, but it had taught me how to fight in a political bout.

On a hot morning in June 1932, my husband, Sam, my political adviser Dan Talbott, and I set out for Chicago and the National Democratic Convention. We drove north through Indiana and Illinois over bad roads that made the trip seem endless. The two-lane highways were choked with cars, trucks, and wagons. America was taking to automobiles, but the highways were not keeping pace. Trains crossed the nation carrying passengers and freight, but the automobile industry was surging ahead. People were demanding better roads on which to travel. Dan and I saw the need for a national highway program east, west, north, and south, and we were determined to get such a plank in our party platform.

Arriving in Chicago, we went at once to the hotel assigned our state by the National Committee in Washington. Our rooms were pleasant, and upon arrival, I found a note signed by Jim Farley, Roosevelt's campaign manager, asking me to drop by Roosevelt's headquarters. I went at once to Dan's room and showed him the invitation.

"Fine, fine," Dan commented. "Go, by all means, but don't commit yourself until we have discussed everything. Promise?"

"Of course," I said. "Why don't you come with me?"

"No, I don't think I will go. I'll stay here and wait for your report. Just remember that we aren't pledged to Roosevelt, so don't fall for his or Farley's persuasive charm."

"OK," I said, "I'll go, listen, and say nothing."

As I came out of the room, I saw my old rival Bill Devereaux, another member of the Kentucky delegation, coming down the hall. Stopping me, he inquired, rather coolly, where I was off to and asked even more coldly, "Didn't I see you leaving Dan Talbott's room?"

"Yes," I replied. "I went in to show him my invitation to Roosevelt's headquarters."

Bill's face darkened. "Let me see it," he demanded roughly.

I was startled by his abruptness, but I handed him the Farley note.

"Who do they think they are, asking you and not me? Did they ask Dan?"

"No, not to my knowledge," I answered. "I haven't seen any other invitations, but I am sure there are others who have been asked, Bill." I hesitated. "Don't be angry." I half held out my hand, but he drew away from me and stalked furiously down the hall. I walked along the corridor thinking, "This means trouble somewhere." Little did I know that, before the evening was over, I would have my first quarrel with Dan Talbott.

As I entered the Roosevelt headquarters, I bumped into a round little man whose head was completely bald and whose twinkling brown eyes passed over me quickly. "Whew!" he whistled and turned to another man who was standing with his back to a window, watching the meeting. "Say, Jim, I think it's nice to have the women's vote, don't you? Sort of adds spice to our meetings." He grinned. He introduced himself: "I'm Sam Rayburn of Texas, and this is Jim Farley, Big Jim to us that know and love him." Jim smiled and winked at me.

It was the twinkle in those eyes that had won my heart some months ago, on the day I opened the door of my house to find him standing in front of me. No one knew it, but Jim Farley had already visited me in Kentucky. He was scouring the country looking for young and enthusiastic workers to put together a grass-roots organization for Franklin Roosevelt. Al Smith had suggested my name. Mr. Smith knew I had raised the money for My Old Kentucky Home, and I had worked for him in his presidential campaign.

When Sam Rayburn, who was a congressman from Texas,

finished introducing Jim Farley, he asked me, "And who might you be?"

I replied simply, "Catherine Conner . . . Kentucky."

"Come in, come in," said Farley, "and meet the gang. This is Mr. Garner of Texas, Governor Byrd of Virginia, Jimmy Roosevelt, and Anna, his sister, Governor Roosevelt's daughter." Farley grinned as a tall man unfolded himself from a seat on the sofa. "This is Amon Carter of Texas, owner of the Fort Worth *Star-Telegram.*"

I glanced around a room that suddenly seemed to fill with people. Some I recognized from pictures in the paper, others I had never seen. There was Forbes Morgan, an uncle of Mrs. Roosevelt's, a big, ugly man whose charm soon won me over. And then through the crowd came a man of whom I had heard but had never met. Many turned to look as he bellowed with his foghorn voice.

"I'm Huey Long of Louisiana," he said. "Anyone in here want to see me?"

"Of course," said Farley smoothly, "we all want to see you."

I was overwhelmed! I had moved so fast in politics, from precinct chairman to national committeewoman to this center of power in four years. But, I was keenly aware of Dan Talbott's advice to listen and keep quiet so I listened. The talk swirled fast around me. Pledges were being discussed and suggestions were being made as to how best to contact the delegations that were still unpledged. I was amazed that they talked so freely and openly. They must have thought of me as a friend—and I was—but my delegation was still unpledged, though no mention was made of it to me at this time. I wondered if I was strong enough to beat Bill Devereaux, who was against FDR. I had been for Roosevelt since that night four years earlier when, listening to the radio, I had heard his beautiful voice in Houston, Texas, where he nominated the Happy Warrior, Alfred E. Smith, for president. The magic of his voice was always to remain with me; but at this time, all I could think of was how to get the Kentucky delegation to back Roosevelt. I returned to my room, bursting with plans. Of course, I would have to see what Dan thought about it.

I found Bill Devereaux, Dan, and my husband waiting for me in my room. Dan got up, his face white and his mouth trembling. "Catherine," he thundered, "why did you commit yourself and our delegation to Roosevelt? You can't do that. You haven't the power. It's only through Bill and me that you can do anything. Bill says he talked to someone in FDR's headquarters, and he was told that you had said you would carry the delegation for Roosevelt. He said you even had your picture taken with Jim Farley and Jimmy Roosevelt."

I looked at him gravely. "Yes, Dan, I had my picture taken with Mr. Farley and Jimmy Roosevelt, but I did not make any promise in the name of the delegation. I only told them that I would do what I could, and I expect to do that very thing. Your idol, Governor Byrd, was there, and I think he will be seeing that his delegation will go for Roosevelt after a few ballots."

"You're nuts," said Bill. "Byrd is a candidate himself and half of our delegation is pledged to him, the other half to Melvin Taylor of Chicago. Only you," he sneered, "are for Roosevelt." He stared at me with hate in his eyes. "Now crack your whip and let's see how far you get."

"Bill, you and Dan have helped me, and I have helped you, too." My voice was trembling. "But you don't own me. I will resign from the committee, but I tell you now, FDR is going to get the nomination, and I am going to work for him."

I was frightened. I knew that between them they could ruin my hardware business. I knew my livelihood was being threatened, but I stood up for what I believed. I left the hotel and went to the lakeshore. Walking along that dark and lonely beach, I breathed deeply and felt the tension ease out of my body as I came to a decision. If Roosevelt were nominated, I would give every ounce of my strength to help him get elected. Having decided this, I returned to my room late that night to find Sam asleep, apparently undisturbed. But it was dawn before I closed my eyes.

As I was having my morning coffee, there was a knock on my door. I opened it and found Dan standing there. "Catherine, can you ever forgive me after last night?" he asked. "May I come in? I am so sorry, but Bill had me upset. He had fairly read you out of the delegation before I knew what was happening, my dearest girl."

"Why did he do it, Dan? What is the matter with him?" I asked.

"Only jealousy. Honey, you beat us to the punch by appearing at the Roosevelt headquarters, and now you are the Roosevelt leader in our state. Bill just can't take that. We have lots of work to do as the delegation isn't all set for Roosevelt. But I am with you, and there are lots of them on the fence, so we will go to work. Who did you see over there?"

"Well," I replied, "there was Governor Byrd, who they say has the greatest political machine in the country, and several men from Texas. Oh, lots of people. I wish you had been with me, Dan, because I want you to be the Roosevelt leader for Kentucky, not me."

To swing the convention to Roosevelt, it was going to be necessary to deal with Harry Byrd. As governor of Virginia until 1930, he had developed a strong national organization to support his bid for the presidency. Most of the real work of a convention takes place behind the scenes, and I was present when Jim Farley challenged Byrd.

"Harry," he said, "I have just returned from a tour of the United States, and the Democratic votes are divided between you and Roosevelt. Neither of you can win if both of you stay in the race. Roosevelt has more votes, and if you will withdraw and throw your pledges to Franklin, we can beat the Republicans. Mr. Roosevelt is ill, as we all know. He will serve

one term and then throw his organization behind you in 1936."
He stopped and looked at Governor Byrd.

There was complete silence in the room. Finally, Byrd drew
a deep breath, got up, walked over to Farley, and took his
hand. "I withdraw," he said. "Let's go to work."

Several days later, the 1932 Democratic convention made its
historic decision, and Franklin Delano Roosevelt was chosen
to wear the mantle of the party. This was indeed a momen-
tous occasion—for the first time in history, a candidate of a
political party was flying to a convention to accept a nomination. Air travel was just getting established, so the novelty of
Mr. Roosevelt's flight caught the nation's fancy. It was a great
piece of publicity, and no one doubted Roosevelt's flair for
publicity.

To me, it was the most exciting night of my life. Nothing
after ever equaled its dramatic accents. At six that evening,
Dan called to ask Sam and me to dinner in the Pump Room of
the Ambassador East Hotel. "It's a room you should see," he
said. Its fame had spread over the world. "It's a smart place
where people go to see and to be seen," he explained.

Sam turned to me. "How about it? Do you want to go?"

"I want to be in the convention hall by ten tonight," I
replied.

"Of course," Sam said, "all of us do. But I think it might
be fun to go with Dan."

"Fine," I replied. "Tell him I have my one and only evening
dress with me. And you will wear your dinner jacket, won't
you, Sam?"

"Sure thing . . . it will look just great where I will be sitting tonight in the gallery, won't it?" Sam quipped. "So it's no
go."

"Oh, you don't sit in the galleries tonight, my boy. Look
what arrived a few minutes ago." I held up a white envelope.

Sam walked slowly across the room and picked up the

envelope. Inside were six tickets for a box and a card that said: "Thanks for your untiring efforts on our behalf. We want your husband to have these for himself and his friends. I will be on the platform at ten tonight. Governor Roosevelt will arrive around eleven. A great evening lies ahead." It was signed "Jim Farley."

The Pump Room was aglow with light and color. Many familiar faces were there. At one table, William Gibbs McAdoo of California, President Woodrow Wilson's son-in-law, was sitting with Arthur Krock of the *New York Times*, a Kentuckian whom I'd known when he was at the *Courier-Journal* in Louisville, and Judge Robert Worth Bingham, owner and publisher of the *Courier-Journal,* later to be ambassador to the Court of Saint James during the Roosevelt administration. Ralph Morrison, a man of great wealth from Texas, waved to us from another table, where he was with some men of the press. Alice Longworth and Daisy Harriman, social and political leaders from Washington, D.C., were with some women reporters. Bernard Baruch, financier and adviser to five presidents, and Vincent Astor of the well-known Astor clan had their heads together over a letter Baruch was reading. I wondered if it had anything to do with tonight's affair. The atmosphere was suffused with laughter, food, smoke, and perfume.

As we were shown to our table, I thought what an attractive room it was and how dear Dan was to bring us here. Sam and Dan were as handsome as any men in the room, and I was so proud of them and so excited that I nearly forgot to eat. The dinner was good, but the people surpassed any culinary delight.

"Dan," I asked, "if Mr. Roosevelt wins the election, do you think there is anyone in this room who might be in the cabinet?"

"I imagine nearly everyone in this room will be in the cabinet," he joked. "I don't know," he went on. "They haven't taken me into their consultations. How about you? You're their 'Girl Friday,' aren't you?"

I glanced at him and saw that it still rankled him that I had gone to Roosevelt's headquarters without him, though I knew he remembered that I had asked him to go with me. As it happened, no one in the Pump Room that night was to be in Roosevelt's first cabinet, but there were many who were to be influential. One was Harry Hopkins, a member of the intimate group surrounding the Roosevelts, who did become a cabinet member in 1939. On this night, he was winding his way around the room, lingering at different tables to politic with those he felt were real friends. As I watched Hopkins, with his ever-present cigarette hanging loosely from his lips, weaving his way crablike through the tables, I saw him speak to a man I could not identify. He was Aubrey Williams, whom I knew much later when he was given the important job of chairman of the National Youth Administration.

Harry seemed to progress through the room like a messenger. When he reached our table, he said to me in a tired voice, "They are going to show motion pictures at the hall at ten tonight of Roosevelt boarding the plane at Albany and in flight. Just thought you might want to be there. He's going to delay his flight by a stopover in order for the film to be rushed to us here and shown while we await his arrival."

I introduced him to Sam and Dan, but he didn't make much of an impression. After he left, Dan muttered, "That SOB surely isn't going to be one of Roosevelt's men."

"A sad sack if ever I saw one," Sam replied.

Nevertheless, Hopkins was to take his place as a policy maker and share in whatever glory accrued to Franklin D. Roosevelt.

Dan lowered his brow. I knew that meant he was thinking long and deep. He glanced up and caught me studying him. "You know, Catherine, it's just possible that we have made a mistake."

"What are you thinking?" I asked.

"I'm thinking of witch doctors. I'm wondering if Harry Hopkins is one. I wouldn't want anyone of that caliber as a friend of the leader of this country. I don't want anyone to have the power to mesmerize the president to where he may compromise his morality."

"Morality?" My voice was skeptical. "What on earth are you talking about?"

"I'm talking about a witch doctor's power to influence the philosophy of a political setup. It's dangerous, and your friend Hopkins gives me the feeling of a witch doctor." Then Dan smiled. "But let's don't be serious tonight. Maybe I'm wrong. Anyway, we have nominated Roosevelt and I am going to do my level best to get the man elected. I want to see him capture the imagination of millions of Americans throughout the country. Will the radio and newspapers ever play up Roosevelt's acceptance speech!" he crowed. "I want to see the Republicans try to beat this one."

We were a merry threesome as we left the Pump Room, caught a taxi, and roared off to the convention hall. For me, it would turn out to be a race for a rendezvous with fate, though no such thought crossed my mind on this night. Rather, as we rushed through the hot streets of Chicago, my mind was occupied with Dan's reaction to Hopkins and his remarks about witch doctors. Perhaps I have underestimated Dan, I thought. Perhaps this man's thoughts are deeper than I knew.

I turned my eyes from the street scenes passing outside the taxi window and glanced at Dan riding quietly beside me. We looked deeply into each other's eyes. His gaze was steady and reassuring, but I felt uneasy. I felt I, too, could fit Dan's description of a witch doctor. I had a certain power inside me, and I knew it. Had I not already been responsible for turning the Kentucky delegation toward Mr. Roosevelt? I knew that with power came money, something I had been taught was a source of corruption.

I knew, also, that this night represented a turning point in my life. If I chose to exercise the power I was gaining with Mr. Roosevelt's nomination, I would certainly take a step away from my husband. There was no doubt I was carrying a burden of guilt. There was also no doubt, come hell or high water, that I would take the opportunities offered me. Perhaps, as he looked into my eyes, Dan Talbott knew, too, what I was going to do.

The convention hall loomed before us. Crowds milled around the entrances. As we got out of our cab, Sam turned to the entrance nearest his box. "Good-bye," he waved, "I'll see you after the show is over."

Dan went to the main floor to sit with the Kentucky delegation, and I sat on the platform with the rest of the National Committee. On my left was Governor Byrd and on my right sat Mrs. Borden (Daisy) Harriman, who represented the District of Columbia on the committee.

The platform was filling rapidly, and Jim Farley was pounding the gavel for recognition and order. There was tension in the air. It seemed to emanate from an expectancy that something dramatic and unusual was about to take place.

Governor Byrd leaned over. "I'm glad you came a little early," he said. "I wanted to ask if you would serve on the Democratic Finance Committee." The blush, for which he was famous, spread over his face.

"What would it involve?" I asked calmly, my heart racing.

"Several trips to New York, probably," he replied, "but I'm not sure myself how involved it will be. I know only that Jim Farley asked me to serve as chairman and I've been scouting for prospects to assist me."

"Which women will be on the committee?" I asked.

"I think you will be the only one. How would you like that?" he asked, chuckling slyly as the blush again crept into his face. Then, becoming serious, he put his fingers to his lips.

Jim Farley had turned to survey the platform. His eyes soon came to rest on us. For a moment, he looked directly into my eyes, then he turned back to the crowded hall. He stood a minute in deep reflection before going back to the business at hand.

Raising his hand, he asked for silence and made a brief announcement that a movie was to be run, showing the flight of Mr. Roosevelt to Chicago. The hall quieted, then burst into wild applause as the plane was shown rolling slowly down the runway for takeoff with Roosevelt at the window smiling that famous smile.

Harry Byrd laid his hand on my tense fingers. "Here he comes. God help us all," he whispered. I turned from the movie to look at the governor, wondering if he, too, believed in Dan's witch doctor theory. Thinking of Dan, I raised my binoculars to my eyes and searched for him on the floor. I found him in the Kentucky delegation, talking to Bill Devereaux. Bill was nodding his head and Dan was speaking earnestly. I wondered if Dan was explaining his theory to Bill.

The night drew wearily on. Byrd had left his seat, and Farley had left the platform. The Roosevelt rushes were over and the speeches were becoming dull. The crowd was tired and restless, and even the organ seemed to have run out of tunes.

Senator Alben Barkley from Kentucky was passing down the aisle. He caught my eye and asked me if I would like some coffee. I had grown to love the irrepressible Alben while listening to his impassioned political speeches. I doubted his sincerity but loved his wit. Once I had attended a Democratic meeting in Frankfort where he was the principal speaker. Although I was for the repeal of the Eighteenth Amendment and Barkley was against it, I had to admire his masterful handling of the subject. At the conclusion of his talk in Frankfort, I had followed him to the lobby of the Capitol Hotel and was among a small group of women who surrounded him as he snatched his coat and hat from a chair and rushed to catch a train. From a pocket of his coat tumbled a bottle of bourbon whiskey that smashed to pieces on the marble floor. As the pungent odor floated upward, everyone stood aghast. I looked with amusement at some twenty women with little white ribbons pinned to their coats, emblems of a pledge to eliminate alcohol, all staring at Barkley with hurt bewilderment.

In a flash, he thundered, "You just can't trust these damned Republicans! They did this to me!" Turning to the ladies, he said, "Pardon me for the 'damn.'" He turned on that charm of his, and his eyes twinkled merrily at his own audacity. "You good ladies know that I don't touch the stuff. Why, I'm working for you, and you know that I am your servant, don't you?" As he shook each of them by the hand, his left hand caressed each arm. I watched how they melted into good humor, and as he left them they were voicing indignation at those damned Republicans.

Remembering former meetings and knowing Barkley's wit and humor, I was delighted at the prospect of a chat with him and followed him off the platform. At a counter under the platform, coffee and hot dogs were being served, and women in evening dresses and men in black ties were consuming them as though they were on a picnic. Everyone was tired of waiting and, as Senator Barkley strolled among them with me on his arm, there were many quips. The running question was, "When will *he* get here?" No one seemed to know for sure, but finally Senator Barkley looked at his watch and hurried me back toward the platform.

"Come, Catherine," he said, putting down his cup, into which he had poured a little libation from a small flask in his pocket. "We must hurry. Mr. Roosevelt is due at four-thirty, and it's four-fifteen now."

"You knew all the time when he was to arrive, didn't you?" I asked.

"Yes," replied Barkley. "See, the hall is beginning to fill.

There go Farley and Byrd. Hi, Sam, Jack," he called as Congressmen Sam Rayburn and Jack Garner, both of Texas, hurried by.

"Catherine, you will see the greatest show on earth tonight, my apologies to Barnum and Bailey." He grinned and squeezed my arm. "Good-bye for now. I'll see you later," he added after depositing me in my seat on the platform. Then he rushed for a conference with Farley and others who were running the show.

The long windows of the convention hall began to fill with the blue light of dawn. A cool lake breeze freshened the stale smoky air and faces began to emerge from the crowd. It was at this moment of daybreak that the whisper ran through the hall. "He is here, he is here." The whisper rose to a roar. I stood transfixed, then tears welled up in my eyes. I stole a glance at Governor Byrd, standing quietly by my side, and saw him wiping his eyes. Looking around the platform, I saw that all eyes were shining with tears.

The sight that met our eyes was enough to move hearts of stone. All that could be seen at first were the soles of two feet coming up over the platform. Then the whole figure of the man suddenly appeared triumphantly, head held high and flashing that famous smile. He was supported on each side by his two sons, James and Elliott. As he swayed from side to side on his march down the aisle, everyone became aware of the toll polio had taken on this gallant man.

I stood watching Franklin Roosevelt's slow, majestic progress, my eyes brimming. He turned his head to my side of the platform, and for one brief second he looked at me. My heart began to throb. My first thought was of the witch doctor. Startled, I sat down and, looking at Byrd, saw that he had fallen into a deep study. He sat with his hands gripping the arms of his chair, staring at the floor.

Picking up my binoculars, I searched the main floor for Dan Talbott. I was startled to see him sitting in the same position as Byrd, with the same somber expression on his face. Could they both be thinking of witch doctors? Years later, I found out that both had indeed been looking into the future and were afraid of what they saw. Theirs had been a vision of a changing United States, and they feared the outcome.

It was at this moment that the grand and melodious voice of Franklin Roosevelt rolled out across the great convention hall and, like thunder, across the nation. The United States, confronting a demoralizing depression, responded as a horse does to the flick of a whip on a homeward journey.

The Republicans faced the music and gave ground foot by foot, then inch by inch. The fight was on! The prairies were afire with the flames of change. The farmers, like drowning men, grasped at Franklin Roosevelt. He had the South solidly behind him. Once again, there was hope in the land.

6

First Political Appointment

In September, I received a brief note from Governor Byrd, asking me to attend a meeting of the finance committee to raise money for Roosevelt's campaign for the presidency. The meeting was to be held at the Biltmore Hotel in New York City.

In 1932 we were in the midst of a money panic, and business was going badly. I was fearful that I could not afford the trip, but I called my husband and Dan Talbott into consultation; and after we'd studied the home situation carefully, it was decided that I must go. Dan was very careful to get my promise not to get into trouble by pledging any money, though he told me, "You always promise and then do as you please, so I'll be expecting anything to happen."

"I do promise, honestly, Dan," I said, laughing, as I lifted my right hand.

As he was leaving, Dan glanced at me sharply with his shrewd brown eyes and warned me again to be cautious of the witch doctor. His concern, however, seemed to have shifted from those who might influence Roosevelt to the man himself. "Should he take the great majority of people and feed, clothe, and house them, someone will have to pay the bill and the price may be the forfeiture of the things that have made America great. . . . To the witch doctor, emotions and wishes are more important than facts. I am afraid this man Roosevelt, like the witch doctor, will attempt to preempt the field of morality, and states' rights and individual rights will begin to sink, as the all-powerful state begins to rise." He stopped and grinned. "Lesson one. Learn it well! It may be important."

I arrived in New York on September 6. It was the first time I had been in that great city. As I emerged from the Pennsylvania Railroad Station, the rushing roar of the city struck me with the force of a cyclone. I turned, bewildered by the hustle and bustle, as a taxi pulled up beside me.

"Taxi, lady?"

"Yes. I want to go to the Biltmore Hotel."

"Righto," the taxi driver grinned. "Are you one of those Roosevelt people from out west?" To all people who live in New York, anything outside the city limits is west. I had noticed that he was glancing into the mirror to watch my face. I thought it pretty smart of him to guess, but I had heard how smart these taxi men were so I was not surprised.

"I certainly am for him, and we will carry our state for him, though it's not considered 'out west.' In fact, I think he will carry the majority of the states," I answered.

"Well, I tell you, lady, I'm for him, and I think this city will go for him. By the way," he continued, as we pulled up to the Biltmore, "see that tall man standing in front of your hotel? That's Big Jim Farley, one of the smartest politicians in the country. Big Jim says the Democrats are going to sweep the country. And if Big Jim says that, you can bet it's so. He's a great guy."

We came to a full stop in front of the hotel. "Hi, Mr. Farley," the driver called.

When Jim saw me emerge from the cab, he hurried over and gave the cabbie a slap on the shoulder. Then he turned to me with a radiant smile. "Welcome, Mrs. Conner. Welcome to New York and our headquarters. I suppose you're here for the finance meeting tomorrow afternoon."

"Yes," I said, "and it's so good to see you. How is the campaign coming along?"

"Fine, just fine. All we need now is money—then we'll be off the ground. 'The Boss' is in great shape. He'll want to see you, I'm sure. As soon as you're settled at the hotel, give me a ring and I'll take you to him. By the way, do call Mrs. Roosevelt and make an appointment to see her. She'll want to have a word with you, too."

"I'll certainly do so," I replied, already swept up in the infectious enthusiasm that radiated from Big Jim. "And thanks, Mr. Farley, for being so kind."

He entered an elevator, where he was joined by several other men. "Think nothing of it." He waved to me.

Following my bellboy, I took the next elevator, which was filled with short-haired and mannishly suited women—not what I had expected to see in New York, the fashion center of the country. I wondered if they were working at Roosevelt's headquarters. The elevator stopped at the fifth floor, and an attractive black woman entered. The women embraced her, kissed her, and asked about her trip.

She rolled her eyes at one of them and said, "Honey, you had better get busy. When I was in Nashville, those damned southern women looked at me as though I were poison. I couldn't stay at the good hotels with the white people. And do you know what that wonderful Mrs. Roosevelt did? She wouldn't stay there either. You should have seen her sweep out. Was that hotel clerk ever miffed! Yes, you should have heard her say, 'If my friend can't stay here, neither can I.'" She rolled her eyes and she rolled her hips, giving an imitation of how she had undulated across the lobby of the hotel as she and Mrs. Roosevelt left. The other women burst out laughing, but the woman she spoke to frowned.

"You are a card," said a woman at the rear of the elevator. "We'll show them, once we get elected."

The black woman threw back her shoulders. "Yes sirree,"

she drawled, "their days are numbered. I told Harry Hopkins about it, and he said to take it easy now. But once we had a chance, we'd show the whole damn stuck-up bunch what stupid fools they were. So I'm going to keep on working here and hope that when Roosevelt is elected I can tell that dumb SOB of a hotel clerk to kiss my you-know-what. See you later in the coffee shop. I have to get off here."

Laughing, she stepped off the elevator. The rest of the women got out at the tenth floor, leaving me alone with the bellboy. As I glanced up. I saw him looking at me from under lowered lids.

"You didn't like that, did you, Miss?"

"Like what," I answered sharply.

"I just got the idea you didn't like that high yellow gal and her flip talk," he replied.

"I didn't listen to the chatter. I really don't know what was said," I answered.

"Well, excuse me." He grinned. "I just caught that look on your face when big mouth was blowing off."

Following him down the long, red-carpeted hall, I thought to myself, I really am a very stupid woman. I have much to learn and much growing up to do if my face reveals everything I'm thinking.

Once inside my room, I walked to the window and raised the blind. New York, with all its bustle, all its excitement and glamour, was spread before me. Its roughness, its tenderness, its fame, its sadness, and its glory were shown to me in that one revealing moment. Staring out the window, I felt as though I had just been reborn. This is my city, I murmured to myself. And truly, for me, life was about to begin. Like all miraculous moments, this one was to recede into some inner depth of my being; but as each event came to pass in my life, I was to remember that brief, revealing flash. I had foreseen it all on that first day in New York, standing at the Biltmore Hotel window, watching the September afternoon.

An hour later my phone rang, and a charming voice said, "Mrs. Conner?"

"Yes," I answered.

"This is Eleanor Roosevelt. I called to ask if you would like to stop by my suite on the second floor for a chat—say, around 4:30."

"Mrs. Roosevelt," I gasped, "of course I will, and thank you for calling me personally."

At 4:30 sharp, I paused in the doorway of Mrs. Roosevelt's quarters. A tall blond languidly rose from a couch where she was sitting, chatting with Jim Farley and Forbes Morgan.

"Mrs. Conner, isn't it?" she asked. "I remember you from the Chicago convention. You know these two gentlemen, don't you?" She paused, then spoke again. "Mother is expecting you. She will be here in a minute."

As Jim Farley walked toward me, I looked past him and found myself staring at Forbes Morgan, the ugliest man I had ever seen. But once again I felt his charm, as I had in Chicago, engulfing me like a warm cream bath. This was like meeting people in your living room—nothing like what I had imagined. Here it was restful as well as exciting. And most exciting of all was seeing the door open and Eleanor Roosevelt sweep in. *Her* charm was equaled only by her husband's.

With shy grace, she put out her hand. "Welcome, child," she said laughing. "We women haven't been in politics too long—not long enough to imitate the men, so I keep my quarters here, just as I would in my own home. I wanted a home-like atmosphere where the women who will be coming in to us this fall can have a place to meet our family and make their plans for organizing the campaign. You must feel free to drop by anytime during your stay here," she said, and I did so on several occasions. "I assure you, there will be many interesting things happening around here, enough for you to have many a tale to tell when you return home. It's really such fun, isn't it?"

"Oh yes," I replied, immediately feeling an admiration

for the shy and charming Eleanor Roosevelt. That is, at first she seemed quiet, shy, and almost self-effacing.

Later on, however, in FDR's presidency, I noticed a change in her demeanor. She would often nod her head and say, "I really worked on Franklin for that bill. I am glad I can get so much more now that the Supreme Court isn't so conservative." Then she took up the habit of questioning, wanting to know everything about one's life at home, the conditions of people in the state. I began to have the distinct feeling she wanted to set up her own headquarters in Washington. If anyone praised Mr. Roosevelt, she would change the subject. I truly think she was jealous of his plans for the recovery of our nation from the terrible Depression and wanted people to think of her as "the power behind the throne." She formed a tight-knit group of women around her. When I refused to join, I lost favor with her. But that was down the road.

On the day of my first visit with her, as I was about to leave, there was a commotion at the door, and in came Mr. Roosevelt, Governor Byrd, and the two Roosevelt boys, James and Elliott. Mr. Roosevelt stood at the door, waiting for his chair to be pushed over to him. His handsome face was shining with good humor and his eyes were twinkling. Again, as on the night of the convention in Chicago, my heart went out to him for his gallantry and courage.

"What have we here? Our girl from Kentucky—the baby of the National Committee," he shouted as I crossed the room to shake his hand amid the laughter that went up at my expense. "How long do you plan to stay?" he asked. "For the duration of the campaign, I hope. You will liven up the place; and with women like you, we can pack our enemies in." He threw back his head and laughed.

"Franklin," Eleanor murmured disapprovingly.

"All right, I'll be good," he promised. "Just watch for those other 'birds.'" He glanced at Governor Byrd, who was standing across the room.

"Yes," replied the governor, moving to my side, "you watch for those other birds, but let this one watch out for you."

Forbes Morgan interjected, "I've been asked to drop by Elizabeth Marbury's house, and as she is the Democratic national committeewoman for New York, why don't you come along if you haven't anything better to do. There are always interesting people there. Some, I'm sure, you would like to know."

I was facing a lonely evening and was delighted with the invitation. In a few minutes I found myself being whisked through the busy streets on the way to Sutton Place and the famous house with the red door where Miss Marbury lived.

Forbes and I walked into the library and into a perfect beehive of a cocktail party. Prohibition was in effect in the United States, and good liquor was hard to come by, but Miss Marbury's cellar proved quite adequate.

When Forbes pointed out our hostess to me, I saw she was sitting in a wheelchair. As I was not adept at hiding my feelings, the sharp eyes of Elizabeth Marbury saw the look of pity I did not realize was on my face.

Taking me by the hand, she drew me to a stool at her side. "Didn't you know that I was unable to walk, Mrs. Conner?" she asked. "I know all about you, and, as you are young, I'll give you a bit of advice. Don't ever go to anyone's house unless you make it a point of knowing all about them. It will save you embarrassment and will prove to be of great help someday. It's plain to see you are a country lass." She let out a lusty laugh. "Forbes, be careful of your chick," she called. "She still smells of milk."

It was not said maliciously, but I was blushing at the directness of the attack. As I sat there feeling gauche and naive, a thin, petite woman came over to me.

"Move over," she said. "There's room enough for us both on this stool. You must not mind Elizabeth. She and I are friends and partners in the decorating business these many years, and sometimes she's rough with me, too. But I understand her, and I hope you will try to do so. By the way, let me introduce myself. I'm Elsie de Wolfe."

This party is certainly the undoing of me, I thought to myself. I must look like a half-wit sitting here with my mouth hanging open and blushing. But recovering my calm, I smiled at the delightful woman who had tried to temper Elizabeth Marbury's forward remarks.

"When did you arrive, Mrs. Conner?" she asked softly.

"This morning," I answered.

"Well, dear, you have covered quite a bit of territory in one day. Sometimes it takes years to be received by Elizabeth Marbury. Want to travel on?"

"What do you mean?" I asked.

"Want to get out of this rat race? Come with me to London tomorrow," said Elsie.

I stared at her with something between horror and amazement. "Really, Miss de Wolfe, you quite take my breath away. I have a son and a husband at home, and I have given up my time in order to work for the election of Mr. Roosevelt. Your offer sounds wonderful, but the answer is no. But someday," I continued, "I do believe our paths will cross again."

"I'm sure of it," Elsie replied. "Oh, look who just came in—Amelia Earhart." The famous flyer was tall and angular and seemed to be in a rush. "We've taken her under our wing," Elsie said, "and I must run and talk with her for a few minutes before I leave. Excuse me."

"Yes," I replied. "Good-bye until we meet again." And we did, many years later in Hollywood.

I was soon to learn that Elizabeth Marbury, Ann Morgan (J.P. Morgan's sister), and Elsie de Wolfe put up some of the money for Miss Earhart's last flight. I have often thought of the tragedy of that flight and wondered what really happened to her. Could she have been on a spy mission? I wouldn't be surprised, for it was plain that Marbury, Morgan, and de Wolfe had their fingers into everything.

I awakened the next morning aware of the importance of the eleven o'clock finance committee meeting. In 1928, I had been the second woman to be elected to a prominent party post in Kentucky, and now in 1932, at thirty-two years old, I was the youngest national committeewoman in the United States. Women had been slow to take part in politics, and I was one of the first to step out on the national stage, a deed that was both frightening and awe-inspiring.

As I walked down the long corridor of the Biltmore Hotel toward the room where the meeting was to be held, I was wondering how I could contribute to the party's coffers. A small man who was standing by the door spoke to me.

"Mrs. Conner?" he began. "My name is Gutzon Borglum, and I have designed, and have in my hand, a medallion with the head of Mr. Roosevelt on one side and that of John Nance Garner on the other." Garner was the vice-presidential nominee. "I believe these medallions could be sold for a dollar each, and with my signature on them they could become a 'collectors' item. They could bring in some money for operating expenses of the campaign."

"Have you spoken to other committee members?" I asked.

"Yes," he replied, "I've spoken to each one as they went in, but they didn't seem interested."

I walked into the committee room with Borglum's medallion clutched lightly in my hand. An idea was beginning to form in the back of my mind.

An august group of men was gathered in the meeting room. Governor Byrd of Virginia was presiding. Seated around a long table were Jim Farley, chairman of Roosevelt's campaign, and several people I remembered from Chicago—Bernard Baruch and Vincent Astor of New York, Amon Carter and Ralph Morrison from Texas, Judge Bingham of Kentucky, and more than a dozen others, including Bob Gore, head of a string of newspapers from Chicago to Florida, and Joseph Kennedy of Massachusetts.

I was the only woman in the room, and all were smoking except Governor Byrd, Jim Farley, and me. Soon smoke filled the air and my eyes were stinging. I tried to wipe the tears away, but they continued to flow. Finally, Mr. Farley got up and opened a window, through which streamed cool September air, and my eyes cleared. I thought I caught a glimpse of annoyance among the other men. "Women in politics!" I could almost hear them thinking.

Governor Byrd explained the purpose of the meeting—which, of course, we all knew—and soon the offers of financial help began. Vincent Astor pledged $17,000; Ralph Morrison, $25,000; Amon Carter, $25,000.

Seated at the table, I leaned toward Governor Byrd and whispered, "Back in Kentucky they told me not to offer one cent. The Depression is on and we are all broke, you know. What shall I say when my name is called?"

"I have always found that if I stand up I think better," he replied. "Perhaps, when I call your name, if you stand you will think of something to say."

How right he was! When I stood up I felt the medallion pressing into my hand. Looking at it, I said, "I have just had an idea. When I came into this room, a Mr. Gutzon Borglum gave me a medallion, and I believe I can get the women of Kentucky to sell five thousand at one dollar apiece. We will send you $2,500 and keep the other $2,500 in Kentucky to help finance Mr. Roosevelt's campaign there."

The proposal met with instant approval. Governor Byrd and Jim Farley both suggested I stay in New York until the November election and organize a women's finance committee to sell the medallion in all forty-eight states.

I stayed on, and the women of the United States, with the help of Gutzon Borglum's signed medallion (he and his son were responsible for carving the faces on Mount Rushmore), raised over $1 million for Franklin D. Roosevelt's campaign for his first term as president.

7

The Move to Washington, D.C.

AFTER THE ELECTION of FDR I returned to my home in Bardstown, with the full intention of settling down again into the quiet life. Yet there was a restlessness in me. In New York I had moved in large and important circles, both political and social; and now I was bored with country life. I missed the eight weeks I had spent there, and I missed Harry Byrd, with whom I had spent much of every weekend of those eight lovely autumn weeks. I had fallen in love, and I was ashamed of myself and didn't want my husband or father or mother to know.

After the finance committee meeting, Henry had asked me to have dinner with him. I went gladly to the speakeasy later known as the 21 Club and drank champagne (which I had never tasted before) served in glasses with a fresh peach in the bottom. I couldn't believe I was with this famous Virginia statesman, governor, publisher, farmer. My love sprang from my admiration for his truly great attributes as a thinker, a politician, and a newspaperman, as well as more personal traits—his shy smile, twinkling blue eyes, apple cheeks, and well-known habit of blushing like a kid.

In late February of 1933, Governor Byrd and Jim Farley

invited me to a dinner for members of the finance committee to be held at the Biltmore. Of course I was glad to return. Again I was the only woman present.

Mr. Roosevelt proposed that to raise more money the chairs on either side of him should be auctioned off. It was a hilarious affair. Finally, one seat was sold to Ralph Morrison and the other to Amon Carter, each bringing $2,500.

Mr. Roosevelt told us of some of his plans, and we believed he would be able to carry them out. They included establishment of the Civilian Conservation Corps, the National Recovery Administration, the Agriculture Adjustment Administration, and the Works Progress Administration. He outlined them in a rough way to show us that the New Deal was intended both to restore the economy and to take care of the ill-clothed, ill-fed, and ill-housed.

When the dinner was over, we gathered around President-elect Roosevelt and said farewell to him as a private citizen. I was carrying a beautifully carved jade cigarette box filled with his favorite cigarettes—Camels. It had been given to me by a friend when I was elected Democratic national committee-woman for Kentucky; and, even though I didn't smoke, I had taken to carrying it more as a conversation piece than for any need. As I sat beside him that evening (none of us would really ever know the private man again), he spied the jade box and asked to see it. I gave it to him at once.

He examined it carefully and then whistled. "This is a beauty."

"Please accept it as a personal gift from me," I said. "Keep it always on your desk in the Oval Office while you guide our ship of state through the choppy waters of Depression back to smoother waters."

Holding the box, he flashed me that famous smile and said, "I accept this provided you accept it back when we disagree and fall out."

I quickly agreed to his terms; and while those standing

around laughed, I wondered if such a thing could ever be possible.

The day after the dinner, a chartered plane flew the finance committee to Washington, D.C., where I expected to stay until after the inauguration on March 4. I had never been there; and, as we approached that beautiful city, Governor Byrd leaned toward me and remarked, "From the air rather than the ground is the best way to see Washington."

The committee members stayed at the Mayflower Hotel. That delightful hotel was in desperate financial straits and rooms were very cheap, as were all the rooms in the famous hotels of Washington in 1933.

One morning as I was having breakfast in the dining room, Ralph Morrison of Texas, another member of the finance committee, was breakfasting with some half dozen men at an adjoining table. Seeing me, he got up and came over to my table. "May I sit down?" he asked, looking very grave. Then he gave me the alarming news that Mr. Roosevelt was going to declare a national bank moratorium right after his inauguration. Mr. Morrison asked me how much cash I had with me. When I told him, he said, "Keep it. Charge your hotel bill and catch the evening train for Kentucky. These are going to be bad days for a while. Call your people at home immediately and tell them to get out what cash they have in the bank. This may be a long haul."

I thanked him, and after leaving the dining room, I called my father to tell him what was going to happen. Then at 6:00 P.M., I left Washington on the Chesapeake and Ohio Railroad, bound for Kentucky. When we pulled into the old Seventh Street Station in Louisville, Papa and Dan Talbott were there to meet me.

Dan began speaking the minute he laid eyes on me. "Due to your early warning, most of us have taken care of the cash situation. I notified as many of our friends as possible, but last night some banker friends called to tell me they would be closing shortly—perhaps today."

These were "the best of times and the worst of times." Good because we had hope and faith in Mr. Roosevelt—bad because we were broke!

I returned to Washington in April because I was appointed a special assistant to Harry Hopkins. I was to help set up the departments that would carry out the New Deal programs he and the president were drafting and to serve as a liaison officer between his office and Capitol Hill, lobbying to get some of the legislation Roosevelt proposed through Congress.

When I first started working for Harry Hopkins, I lived at the Mayflower, where I had a beautiful suite of rooms on the eighth floor for $125 a month. Since my salary was only $300, toward the end of the month, I, like many other eager beavers, would run out of money.

It was that great gentleman, Mr. Polio, the manager of the Mayflower, who saved the day. Along about the twenty-fourth of the month, he would invite five or six of us to have dinner in the kitchen. From those stoves in the basement of the Mayflower Hotel came the most delectable steaks, roasts, and salads.

Of course, those of us who were privileged to dine on such cuisine couldn't help bragging, and finally we each began to bring a guest, then just one more, until our group far outgrew the original table. Mr. Polio was soon obliged to issue tickets to the original six. We were the only ones allowed below stairs. This, too, stopped when summer came and we began to branch out. But I'll always remember the wonderful Mr. Polio and how he helped a very hungry crew.

These were the gray days of early 1933. The United States was broke; government, business, and the people were fright-

ened. The banks were taking stock of their assets and the ordinary investors were holding their breath and praying that
President Roosevelt would keep his promises.

I had an occasion to remember such a promise. In the
previous year, a Kentucky man by the name of Seldon Glenn
had been promised the job of collector of internal revenue for
the state. After months of his getting the run-around from
well-intentioned but careless politicians, his appointment had
not come through. I was contacted in Washington and asked
if I thought I could be of any help. I replied that I would try to
redeem the promise from Mr. Roosevelt.

I called Marvin McIntyre, Mr. Roosevelt's appointment
secretary and a native of Kentucky, to ask for an appointment
with "the Boss." He made it and called me with the day and
hour that President Roosevelt would see me.

As I walked into the lobby of the White House that rainy,
dull afternoon and saw many businessmen, bankers, and politicians sitting dejectedly, my heart fell. How could I go into
that office, the heartbeat of the United States, with a trivial
request for a job for an ordinary man?

Nevertheless, I had to do what I could when my political
friends called me. When I entered Mr. Roosevelt's office, he
looked up with that jaunty grin of his and held out his hand.
"Well," he inquired, "what brings you out on such a rainy
day, and looking so sad, too?"

"Oh, Mr. Roosevelt," I burst out, "I am appalled that I
dared to come in with my little problem when the whole world
is depending on you. Let me leave and I'll put off my affairs
until sometime later."

"Just a minute, my child," he answered, "sit here." He
patted a chair drawn up close to the side of his desk. Squirm-
ing around, he pulled a crumpled pack of Camels from his
back pocket. I glanced at my jade cigarette box resting on his
desk. He saw the look and answered my unspoken question.
"Those are for strangers, all fresh and nice, but these are for

my good friends." He offered me one. Naturally, as I didn't smoke, I declined.

"Now, what is your problem?" he asked. I explained about Seldon Glenn and the appointment that he was supposed to have received, and I wept into my handkerchief.

"Well," said Mr. Roosevelt, "I don't want you weeping over broken promises. I'll see Jim Farley, and I want you to know that as long as I sit in this chair, your problems are my problems. All of America's problems are mine," he ended.

Some weeks later, Jim Farley called to tell me Mr. Glenn's appointment had gone through with FDR's initials on it.

While I was Harry Hopkins's assistant I was on the Hill nearly every afternoon, and sometimes I would run into Vice-President Garner. Jack Garner was one of the most lovable men in politics and one of the smartest. Those who saw the prickly side of him called him "Cactus Jack," but I never saw that side.

Mrs. Garner was his secretary, and she didn't like to see him using alcohol. She would find his bottle and confiscate it until he devised hiding it in the toilet tank. She never found it there!

Around five o'clock in the afternoon, he usually gathered up some of his cronies—Sam Rayburn, now Speaker of the House; Harry Byrd, who had been appointed in March 1933 to fill out a Senate term and retained that seat until 1965; Millard Tydings and others—and we would all go to Mr. Garner's office. There he would lead us into his innermost sanctum sanctorum, get out paper cups, and reach down into the toilet tank for the beloved bottle. Then he would pour us a small libation, raise his paper cup, and give a toast to striking a blow for liberty. We would all stand and drink our allotment in great solemnity. Then would begin the stories and jokes of the day.

Mrs. Garner always looked very disapprovingly at us as

we backed out of her office, giving her our gayest good-byes. One day she stopped me as I was on my way into the inner sanctum.

"Catherine," she whispered, "do you know where he keeps the stuff?"

"No," I lied, "he usually has poured my drink by the time I get there." She just looked at me. Then, shaking her head, she went on with her work.

Really, Mrs. Garner was most tolerant; but one day we found ourselves in trouble. Harry Byrd brought in applejack made from apples out of the famous orchards at his estate, Rosemont. None of us was familiar with the stuff. It tasted so good we all had seconds. And that was it! As we staggered out of Mrs. Garner's office, she became furious with her husband and all of us. After berating us for about five minutes, she pointed a dramatic finger at the vice-president.

"And you," she intoned, "will pay for this. You'll be sick and I won't help you, so help me God!"

It was a few weeks before the sessions started again.

Sam Rayburn, longtime U.S. representative from Texas, had become Speaker of the House soon after Mr. Roosevelt was elected. The Speaker of the House is more important than the vice-president (unless the president dies) or the Senate leader. He wields enormous power and is respected, feared, and followed.

One morning Sam called me and said he was leaving that afternoon for New York to address the National Association of Manufacturers and would probably see some of my friends. Would I like to send any messages? I would and did.

The National Association of Manufacturers, with its wide business ramifications, was one of the most powerful and important associations in the country. Sam had always been a true friend to the group, very helpful in putting through beneficial legislation.

About six the next afternoon, my friend Jim Bruce, vice-president of National Dairies, called and gave me the following account of the event.

He said Sam arrived, was greeted enthusiastically, and before and during dinner was most affable and friendly. After dinner the speeches began. Each manufacturing company was represented by its president or vice-president, and all had tales of woe about how they were being discriminated against by President Roosevelt's programs. They appealed to Sam to find some relief for them in Congress.

Jim said Sam sat there listening with a pained expression on his face, his eyes downcast. Finally the president of the association called on Sam to reply to their anguished appeals, and Sam rose to his feet twirling his fraternity key around his finger.

"Gentlemen," he said, "This meeting reminds me of a Negro baptizing I went to once back home in Texas. A little boy was led out into the creek, and the black parson clapped a handkerchief over his eyes and ducked him, back side down, deep into the water. As the parson raised the child, he called out in ringing tones, 'Do you believe, boy?'

"'Yes'r, I believe,' said the boy.

"The preacher ducked the boy again and, upon raising him out of the water, cried out in an even louder voice, 'You believe, boy?'

"'Yes'r, I believe,' quavered the boy.

"The preacher did it a third time and this time he roared, 'DO YOU BELIEVE?' as he raised the now thoroughly frightened boy.

"At that moment, a voice was heard from one of the congregation gathered on the bank of the creek. 'What do you believe, boy?'

"The boy rolled his eyes and shouted, 'I believe this son of a bitch is tryin' to drown me!'"

Jim roared as he told me the story. He said the association

members realized they were putting too much pressure on Sam Rayburn, and their respect and affection for him grew even more.

In 1933, the Soviet Union was given official diplomatic standing, and I was invited to the opening of their embassy. We of the New Deal, who had been living austerely, were bewildered by the lavishness of the event.

The most gorgeous array of food and wine I had ever seen or tasted was served that evening. The dining rooms were filled with large, steaming silver platters, from which rose the most exotic and tantalizing odors. Candles and subdued lights made a soft, sparkling background for the hundreds of people who had received the ornate invitations to communist Russia's first attempt at socializing in Washington, D.C.

I remember talking to Mrs. Roosevelt about going to the reception. I asked her what to wear. She replied, "The most beautiful dress you have or can find. Be sure, they will have an *out of this world* party. They are like that. The Russians of today haven't the polish or elegance of the Russians of old, but they would have the world think they are up-to-date."

Taking her advice, I flew to New York to buy a dress. I found a beautiful red damask satin, a classic I kept for decades. I'm afraid I'm not very subtle. To recognize the Reds, I wore red. In fact, I was the only one there in red.

In March 1934, when President Roosevelt made it a policy that no one serving on the Democratic National Committee could hold a position in government, some people dropped off the committee; but I was the only one who instead resigned my government post and stayed on the committee. This caught the fancy of the newspapers in New York, Washington, and Philadelphia, and they wrote about it. Within a few weeks, I had more than ten clients paying me to keep them posted on what was going on in Washington that would affect their interests. Thus, a public relations firm, Conner Associates, was founded. Among my clients were National Dairy Products, General Foods, Austin Powder Company (a subsidiary of DuPont), International Aviation Corporation, and Borden.

Even though I was now living in Washington, I periodically went back to Kentucky to see my family. My mother and father had sold the farm and moved into the little cottage near the town square where Sam and I had first set up housekeeping. My father enjoyed easy access to the courthouse, where he and his cronies sat, whittled, and caught up on the town gossip. He owned a commercial building on the town square, in the basement of which he set up a bar and a table for his weekly poker games.

I couldn't see it then, but our son Jimmy—doubtless because I was away so much of the time—was growing closer and closer to his father. Sam and I had reversed our parenting roles. I was in Washington making extraordinary money and exercising opportunities to help my friends back home, and Sam was home rearing Jimmy. It was no wonder their bond grew so strong.

8

My Most Famous
Dinner Party

I WOULD NEVER HAVE GIVEN the dinner party if I hadn't taken the house in Georgetown; and I would not have taken the house if it hadn't been for Swing Low, a Chow puppy sent to me by a friend in New York. What that dog cost me!

I was living at the Mayflower Hotel, enjoying my public relations work with no complications when Swing Low arrived. I had not known I was going to be the recipient of such a gift; so when I walked into my apartment one afternoon and saw a baby's playpen in the middle of the floor with a tiny blond Chow puppy backed up in a corner of it, I was astonished and pleasantly surprised.

At our first meeting I fell in love with the puppy, but my love was not instantly returned. Every time I approached the pen, she growled—and what a fierce growl from such an adorable baby. Later that night, when I was awakened by the soft whimpering of the lonesome pup, I went into the living room and reached down for her and she came to me like a baby. I took her into my bed, where she snuggled down and slept the night away. In fact, she slept with me every night from then until she died a year later.

Swing Low—called that because she had the cutest little

rounded bottom that swung close to the ground—changed my whole way of living. Hotel life was not for her. The bellboys were her slaves, but Swing would have none of them. Every time they took her out for walks she nipped their ankles or their hands if they tried to pet her. But so deep was their devotion to Swing that they would come back to the apartment laughing and bragging about "that little devil's sharp teeth."

Swing was afraid of the revolving doors in the lobby, and her performance at the doors usually attracted crowds. She would squat on her haunches until the doors stood perfectly still, then she would spring at them like a cat springs at a mouse. It was always very funny to watch, and the boys loved to see her go into her act. She also had the habit of lying on the windowsill of my eighth-floor apartment, watching the traffic below with such a lonesome air that I decided I had better get a house with a garden so that she could have more freedom.

I found a beautiful old house in Georgetown that was owned by General Douglas MacArthur and his first wife. They were getting a divorce and wanted to rent the house. I sent at once for Hawk to come and bring the car I had left in Kentucky. I had not felt the need for a car in Washington, but now an automobile seemed a necessity. Hawk's coming and working for me as both chauffeur and butler was the answer to my problem.

On moving day, a lovely day in the early spring of 1934, Hawk arrived at the hotel quite early. Swing, who had a memory of a frightening ride by taxi from the airport to the hotel upon her arrival in Washington, was scared to death. She howled like a banshee and clung to me with her head buried in my shoulder. Finally, Hawk and the bellboys got us into the car, and we were able to leave.

Arriving at our new home, I took Swing directly to the garden, which she immediately appropriated as her own. No matter how many bulbs were secreted in the small garden's border, Swing found and dug them up and replaced them with her bones and little toys.

Now that I had taken the house, I found my social life stepped up several notches. Invitations to dinners and cocktail parties began to pour in. The lovely old house was three stories tall, beautifully furnished, and came with a cook and a gardener; so here I was with a Washington house to worry about, servants to guide and direct, and an ever-increasing workload to handle.

Upon learning that I had acquired a house, clients of my public relations firm began asking if they might meet people through the medium of the dinner party. To satisfy their demands, I took on the added duties of giving small fetes, to which were asked, not only my own friends, but also business prospects my clients wanted to meet in a social atmosphere.

I had given three such dinners and had gotten the procedure so well organized that things were pretty routine by the time I gave what came to be known in Washington as the Funniest Dinner of the Year. I remember every detail: the dress I wore, the menu, the whole dreadful night. The guests were asked for 8:00 P.M., with dinner to be served at 8:30 P.M. Cocktails, as usual, were served at 8:00 P.M., the extra time a grace period for late arrivals.

At 7:15 on this particular evening, I floated down the stairs to find Hawk leaning disconsolately on the newel post at the foot of the stairs. "What is the matter?" I asked sharply. One look at Hawk's face convinced me that something had gone dreadfully wrong.

"There ain't a one of our regular waiters showed up, Miss Catherine," he said.

"Gracious goodness alive," I shouted, going into immediate action. "You go over to Mr. Jimmy Roosevelt's house"— Jimmy lived across the street—"and see if we can borrow his butler. I'll call the Mayflower to see if Eric, the headwaiter, can send a couple of waiters."

Hawk flew into action; but as he left, he stopped in the kitchen and, unbeknownst to me, sent the cook to see whom she could round up, leaving me with no one in the house.

I hit the telephone and called my friend Eric at the Mayflower. I explained my predicament, and he promised to see what he could do. Then he suggested that I call Mr. Moore, the manager of the Sheridan Hotel, and Bob Dove at the Carleton to see if they could help. I called them, and they both promised to do what they could, but I was frantic!

It was now eight o'clock. What on earth would I do if my guests arrived and there was no one to serve dinner?

I reviewed my guest list—it included the courtly and handsome secretary of state, Cordell Hull, and Mrs. Hull; Jerome Frank, one of the group known as Roosevelt's "Brain Trust"; Evelyn Peyton Gordon, a newspaperwoman in Washington whose peppery tongue usually made a mixed dinner of Democrats and Republicans a lively evening; Sam Rayburn, Speaker of the House, whose bald head contained so much wisdom, wit, and sympathy, an addition to any party; pretty Marguerite (Missy) LeHand, personal secretary to President Roosevelt; Kentuckian justice Stanley Reed of the Supreme Court and Mrs. Reed; Jim Bruce, tall and handsome vice-president of National Dairies, down from New York for the night; Alben Barkley, jovial storyteller and senior senator from Kentucky; Celeste Miller from Warrenton, Virginia, whose lovely old home there had been the scene of many a famous house party of distinguished men and women from all over the world; Senator Millard Tydings of Maryland and his wife Eleanor, who, wearing her famous emerald necklace, would be the object of all eyes; Harry Hopkins, who, with a cigarette dangling from the corner of his mouth, as usual, would be the center of a group discussing the New Deal and FDR; Mrs. Hopkins; and Mildred Chandler, wife of the Kentucky governor, A. B. Chandler.

A 1912 family portrait of Catherine Anne Conner (second from left, middle row) surrounded by various relatives of her mother, Nancy Hayes Rouse (far left, back row).

(Unless otherwise noted, photographs are from author's private collection.)

Right, A 1962 portrait of the author's mother, Nancy Hayes Rouse, at age eighty-three.

Left, Catherine Conner's father, James Valandingham Rouse.

Above, Eleanor and Franklin D. Roosevelt. Conner, who first met the Roosevelts at a 1932 campaign finance committee meeting, believed that Eleanor wanted to be "the power behind the throne." *Below,* Among Conner's political acquaintances were Franklin D. Roosevelt, Speaker Sam Rayburn, and Majority Leader Alben Barkley, shown here in the 1941 inauguration parade.

Left, Conner's friend Samuel Rossof at Saratoga Race Course. Rossof, who received contracts in excess of $40 million to build New York City subways, was deemed "a character, an eyeful and a local wonder" by the *New York Times*. Photo courtesy Keeneland-Cook.

Right, Conner and her beloved chow, Swing Low, in Washington, D.C., in the mid-1930s.

Left, Catherine's son, James Daniel Conner, who died in 1963 at the age of forty-two. Conner writes that her "only truly happy days" were given to her by Jimmy.

Below, Tired of the "lazy party life" of Hollywood, Conner (front row, center) gave greater attention to public service. In addition to serving on the United Nations Day Committee, Catherine worked with Jimmy Stewart (far right) for the American Cancer Society.

Left, Conner and her mother, Nancy Hayes Rouse, at a restaurant in Reno, Nevada, in 1948.

Below, Conner strikes a pool-side pose at her Bel Air home in the late 1940s.

Above (left to right), Harry Adams, Catherine Conner, Mildred and
"Happy" Chandler, and Mrs. Adams. As governor of Kentucky,
Chandler appointed Conner to the Tourism Bureau. *Below,* A 1957
article on Conner's efforts to promote Kentucky tourism called her
"a woman of intelligence, charm, and beauty." Photo courtesy *The
Courier-Journal.*

Catherine Conner in 1990.

I had planned to seat Mrs. Chandler next to Jerome Frank, knowing they would be the life of the party and would send Evie Gordon into a tizzy. The evening had held such promise, but it threatened to become a nightmare. What would the morning papers say? I could imagine the society column.

I was horror-stricken. For the first time in my life, I lost all contact with reality. I was in shock. I stood frozen in the hall while Swing Low cried at my feet in an agony almost as intense as my own. She was such an understanding little dog. If I were worried and nervous, Swing would pace the floor in a perfect turmoil until I calmed down; tonight she knew that disaster had struck. She could do nothing but offer me the sympathy of suffering by my side.

My lovely house was constructed in an English style with the entrance on the ground floor, the drawing room and dining room on the second floor, and the bedrooms and library on the third floor. As Swing and I stood rooted in the hallway, I heard the doorbell ring. I waited a full minute while Swing crouched at my feet, looking anxiously between the banisters toward the front door. There was no movement in the house. Hawk had not returned! Again, I heard the peal of the doorbell, and I was spurred into action. I ran down the stairs and opened the front door. There stood a very handsome young man—later, he told me he had been a little taken aback by my appearance, because he knew that it was not customary in Washington for the hostess to answer her own door.

When I demanded, "Who are you?" he seemed frightened, but gave me his name and told me that he was there at the suggestion of columnist Drew Pearson. Ah, yes, I remembered the call from Drew, beseeching me to ask this man to one of my dinners. And, oh dear, I had asked him to this one! Without further ado, I blurted out the whole story.

"I can't even find my own cook and butler—they have both disappeared," I wailed. "What on earth am I going to do?" At that very moment, looking over his shoulder, I saw a taxi draw up and Evie Gordon preparing to disembark.

"Here," said my guest, who was Russian, "take my hat and I will open the door for your guests. No one knows me, and I will play the butler. I'm sure your own butler will return shortly."

Time was running out so I grabbed his hat and flew up the stairs to take my place just outside the drawing room door, where I always received my guests. At once, Evie's head appeared; as she came up the stairs, she was smiling. "Catherine," she gasped, "who on earth is that man at your door? Your new butler? And where is Hawk? The new man is really something. Do you imagine those smoke pearls he's wearing are real?"

She fired the questions at me so quickly I couldn't get a word in edgewise. "Stop it, Evie," I cried. "I'm in the most dreadful trouble." Then I poured out the story to her.

Evie threw back her head and roared. "Well, you have done it, haven't you? This will be the funniest dinner party of the year, I promise you." And in her column the next morning, it became just that.

She left me for the drawing room just as my new "butler" announced Justice and Mrs. Reed. Guests followed in quick succession, and when Alben Barkley came up, he said, "Are you having the Ethiopian ambassador tonight?"

"No," I answered, puzzled. "Why do you ask?"

"Well, a tall black man in full evening dress came in right behind me, and I wondered if he were a guest," Alben replied with his usual hearty laugh. Then he went on to speak to Justice and Mrs. Reed, old friends of his from Kentucky.

My heavy heart was relieved. The crack about the "Ethiopian ambassador" was intended to mean Hawk, who had at last returned.

In a very few minutes, Hawk entered with cocktails, and as he passed me he gave me one of his glowering looks and whispered out of the side of his mouth, "Don't worry, I got him. He won't move 'til I get around to taking care of him."

I stared at Hawk and wondered what on earth he was talking about, but guests were claiming my attention, and his remark passed out of my mind until a half hour later. Then I had reason to remember what he had said.

At 8:30 sharp, dinner was announced. As I walked into the dining room, I felt my face turn red with embarrassment. There, lined up one man behind each chair, was the strangest assortment of waiters I had ever seen. Some were black, some white, Italian, Greek, Filipino, some tall, some barely coming to the top of the chairs behind which they stood, and all dressed in the uniforms of the different hotels from which they had come. My hotel friends had done well by me—but how awful they looked in my dining room!

My guests took one look and, mellowed by Hawk's famous old-fashioneds, tried hard to hide their amusement. They must have thought I was giving a fun dinner and that everything was done for laughs, but that certainly had not been my intention. By this time, however, I was riding with the events, taking everything that happened with a laugh. It seemed the evening had gotten out of hand and, like a trolley off the rails, was rolling along—but not on the track. My guests couldn't hide their feelings and were smothering their laughter behind their hands.

As we were being seated, I noticed one empty chair. I blinked my eyes. Surely I was seeing things. I knew I had counted the guest list too many times to be mistaken, but still there was that one empty chair. At this moment Hawk whispered in my ear, "Miss Catherine, I got that sneak thief cornered downstairs. He was trying to pretend he was a butler, but I sure got onto him in a hurry. Want me to call the police?"

"Hawk," I gasped, "that's the missing guest! Get him quickly."

Hawk turned pale. "Oh, my God," I heard him mutter as he rushed from the dining room.

When he returned with the missing guest, the Russian had a wild and glassy look in his eyes. He seemed afraid of everyone. Later he told me he thought he had gotten into an asylum by mistake and the famous people he saw arriving must be there for a board meeting.

After he had been introduced to everyone and assured that no harm was intended—that he was merely the victim of a horrible oversight—he told us the story of his brief incarceration below the stairs. He said that Hawk had run at him, brandishing a poker, and threatened him with instant annihilation if he moved from the spot on which he stood. So he stood perfectly still in the hall for nearly half an hour. "Truly," he said, "they were the most fear-filled minutes of my life."

Of course, this sent my guests into gales of laughter. Senator Barkley said, in telling it afterward, "Honestly, it was the gayest, maddest dinner I ever attended."

As I was in the midst of telling the guests at my end of the table how it all came about—the assorted waiters and the Russian butler—I heard a loud crack that would still any woman's heart with fear, especially if her dining room were filled with someone else's priceless antiques. A chair had given way! Turning, I saw Sam Rayburn disappear under the table. This is it, I thought. This is the end. I'm going to have hysterics!

Of course I did not have the relief of having hysterics—that would have been too easy. The dining room was long and narrow, difficult to maneuver in, and everyone had suggestions for extricating Sam. Someone suggested that all the guests get up so that the waiters could move the table. I vetoed this idea because I was afraid the table would break if we tried to move it, loaded as it was with crystal and silver. To undress the table would have ended the dinner, and we had only finished the soup course.

I could hear Senator Barkley at his end of the table chuckling to his neighbor that the evening was living up to every expectation. Even the dignified Cordell Hull was convulsed. He usually had a very dry sense of humor, and I had never seen him laugh so long and hard. After the explosion of laughter, we could hear Sam under the table speaking plaintively.

"If everyone will be quiet a minute, now that I have the floor, I would like to make a speech."

Again we burst out laughing. Even the waiters joined in and were holding their sides.

"Order!" rapped Senator Barkley. "The house will please come to order. Anyone causing any unseemly outbursts from the gallery will be asked to leave." Motioning to the waiters, he said, "Attendants, see that my rule is obeyed."

Again everyone howled, and from under the table came the voice of Sam Rayburn. "Senator, do I have the floor now?"

"You certainly do," replied Senator Barkley. "Proceed, Mr. Speaker."

Sam replied, "Now that I have the floor, I wish to thank Senator Tydings for yielding to me. When I last saw him, he was being very charming to the lovely Mrs. Reed. Now, from where I am, I shall try to identify the ladies by their legs. Some have discarded their shoes, and from the looks of their poor, pinched toes, I don't blame them."

The women began to tug at their skirts and, at each identification, blushed.

Sam rose to the occasion with the natural-born instinct of a politician. "That Eleanor Tydings has a real classy pair of gams and a corn. Sorry, honey, they sure can hurt. I wish it were my feet instead of my you-know-what. I just didn't sit down gently, you know. Mrs. Hull, well, I won't discuss your stockings. I am sure you are aware of the run, so I will pass on to Mrs. Conner, who, bless my soul, doesn't even have on stockings."

At this point, I decided it was high time I led Sam from his hideout. So I, too, crawled below and directed him to the end of the table nearest the door. We both emerged on our hands and knees. By then, everyone was limp and exhausted from laughing.

Sam was the last to leave the party that night, and as he left, I noticed him rubbing the back of the hip upon which he must have fallen.

9

Public Relations

ONE OF MY CLIENTS WAS the Austin Powder Company, a DuPont subsidiary. I had worked with Austin since my highway construction experience in Kentucky and I did sales as well as public relations. That was how I met Sam Rosoff at the Waldorf-Astoria Hotel in New York in 1935.

The home office had brought to my attention that Rosoff had been awarded a contract for constructing subways in New York City and suggested that I get in touch with him to see what part of his purchase in explosives and cement we could garner.

To me, Rosoff was just a name, one I had never heard of until the company called me about him. But I was sure that my friend Jim Farley, postmaster general at this time and a resident of New York, would either know him or know of him. Acting on this hunch, I called the U.S. Post Office and made an appointment to see Mr. Farley. Two days later my appointment came through.

On the morning of my appointment, Washington lay lovely and serene in the May sunshine, and I was happy with the world. As I drove along the Potomac, I began to wonder what Sam Rosoff was like. My work led me into so many offices, and I met so many people that I had taken to speculating about their nationality, their looks, and their character. I had heard or read of many, but Rosoff was a complete mystery.

I was shown into Mr. Farley's sumptuous office immediately upon my arrival. Jim, in his usual genteel fashion, got up from his desk and walked the length of the room to greet me.

At six foot three, Jim Farley was a very handsome man. His body was well proportioned and he carried his years lightly. His even temper and his general liking for people made him look as happy as he was. In my opinion, it would be hard to make Jim Farley mad, but if one ever succeeded, I wouldn't have wanted to be around. Jim was one of the best-loved men in the country, and many men and women in all walks of life were proud to call him friend.

He escorted me to his desk and asked about his many friends in Kentucky. I told him that I hadn't seen his old friend Dan Talbott since Christmas but that I kept in close touch with most of our political friends. My ties back home at this time were very close—I was, of course, still Democratic national committeewoman—and we Democrats were riding high.

"Tell me," Jim said, "why am I favored with this early morning visit? What do you want, Catherine? I know you didn't come down here just to see my shining blue eyes." And his eyes were shining, indeed, as he looked me over.

I told him that my company wanted me to get in touch with Sam Rosoff from New York and that since I didn't know Mr. Rosoff, I had come to him for advice.

"Well, you have come to the right place and the right man. Sam is a great friend of mine, personally and politically. He is a Democrat and a hero worshiper. FDR is a man above all men to him. I don't know how you and Sam will hit it off. He certainly isn't your type of man." He paused. "Yeah, you and Sam may just hit it off; and if you two should make a go of it, you will certainly profit from knowing him."

Jim drummed on his desk for a moment, then he called Bill Bray, his secretary. "Bill, see if you can find Sam Rosoff in New York, please."

"Yes, sir, Sam Rosoff coming right up," Bill replied with a big grin, and then he disappeared into his own office. Just a few minutes later, Jim's phone buzzed.

Taking up the receiver, he said, "Sam, you old son of a gun, how are you?" Jim listened for several minutes. I could hear a guttural voice on the other end of the line. Then Jim said, "We'll go into that some other time, but now I want to introduce a young lady who wants an appointment with you. How about giving her one in the next day or two? Okay? That's fine." He turned and handed the phone to me.

"Mr. Rosoff," I began hesitantly.

"Come—come, now," boomed the loudest voice I had ever heard. "Youse musta not put the Mr. Rosoff to me. If you friend of Mr. Farley, you friend of mine. Call me Sam. You come tomorrow to see me eleven o'clock in the morning, eh?"

He paused, and I thought he was hanging up on me.

"Yes—yes, but where, Sam?" I cried.

"Where?" he asked. "Why, here, of course. Here at my suite at Waldorf. Some plush place, eh?"

I turned to look at Jim, but before I could say another word I heard a harsh, "Bye, now," and the phone crashed in my ear. I looked at Jim in bewilderment. "What do you know," I murmured.

Jim burst out laughing. "Don't say that I didn't warn you," he said. "Be sure to call me if you need any help in New York. Sam is a diamond in the rough if there ever was one." Jim shook his head. "Leave it to you to locate it."

As I left, I saw Jim studying me, and I wondered if I would get along with this "diamond in the rough." When I reached the door, Jim said, "You know, I'd give anything to be at that meeting tomorrow. It may make history."

Even in Bill Bray's office, I could still hear Jim laughing.

By now, I was anxious to meet Rosoff. I paused at Bill's desk. "Bill," I asked, "what dialect does Rosoff speak?"

"Sam is the salt of the earth," Bill replied. "But to answer your question, he speaks English with a Polish, Russian, and Jewish accent; and he is as quick as lightning with figures, so be on your toes when you see him and be sure you know what you're talking about. You can bet your bottom dollar *he* will."

I thanked Bill and left to hurry home and get packed to leave for New York that afternoon. I called the home office of Austin Powder for last-minute instructions and left Washington well fortified with facts and figures.

Having spent a restful night at the Plaza, my usual stopping place in New York, I left the hotel at 10:30 sharp for my date with Rosoff at the Waldorf. I called his apartment from the lobby and was told by a deep basso voice that Mr. Rosoff wanted to know who was calling. I announced myself as Catherine Conner from Washington, calling at the suggestion of Mr. Farley. In just a second Sam was on the phone. "Come right on up, sweetheart," he breathed softly into the phone. "I'm expecting you."

As I left the elevator, I suddenly had misgivings. Was I going to this man's business office or his private apartment? Yet I knew that Jim Farley wouldn't have sent me if Sam Rosoff was a man on the make. Still, I was worried; and when I rang the bell of his apartment, I admitted to myself that I was scared. There stood a big, hulking man who stared at me with such a burning look that I drew back.

"Mr. Rosoff?" I questioned.

"No, lady," said the same basso voice I'd heard on the phone. "Do come in, please. Mr. Rosoff will be with you in a minute."

I walked in and, as I crossed the living room, saw out of the corner of my eye a ponderous man about five feet eight, dressed in a flaming red dressing gown with a vivid green scarf tucked around his neck. His fat feet were padding toward me in brown mule house slippers. His coarse face was full with nostrils flared above a generous mouth. His glasses were halfway down his nose, and he was peering at me over the top of them with a half leer, half grin. I was really frightened now!

"Come in, sweetheart, come in," he shouted, and I recognized the voice from the day before.

I backed away, startled, and began in my coldest and most dignified voice. "I expected to see you at your office, as I am here on business and," I glanced at his attire, "and it's not monkey business, either."

"Now, child, don't get upset," said Rosoff, with a very different inflection. "Old Sam couldn't have such a nice lady come to his dirty office downtown. But this here," he waved his arms wide and smiled the sweetest smile I have ever seen on a man's face, "why, this here, my uptown office, is where I see lady like yourself and gentleman like Jim Farley. You forgive old Sam his dressing gown, eh? Now, we settle down to business, what say?" Again he smiled that strange smile that I will always remember.

I sat with Sam Rosoff until two that afternoon. The lunch he ordered was served with dignity and with the aplomb of a connoisseur from the old school. We hashed out all the business angles, and as I prepared to leave, he assured me that a big slice of the business I had come for was mine. I knew my company would be delighted, and I was overjoyed. Expressing my thanks, I stood to leave.

Sam put a pudgy hand on my arm. "Mrs. Conner," he said, "would you do me the honor of having dinner with me tonight?" He paused expectantly. Seeing my hesitance, he again brought out that sweet smile. "Don't you think I deserve that much for a big order?"

"Mr. Rosoff, you are a grand guy," I said. "Of course, I'd be delighted to go to dinner with you."

"Very well, I will pick you up at eight sharp," he replied with great dignity.

I walked from the Waldorf to the Plaza, thinking deep thoughts. As soon as I reached my hotel, I phoned Mr. Farley in Washington. When he answered, I told him the whole story, including the dinner invitation.

"Do go, by all means," Jim said. "I told you he was an all right person, didn't I? It seems to me you two hit it off, and I'm glad."

I hung up, feeling pleased with the day and, to my surprise, looking forward to the evening.

Promptly at eight, my phone rang and the doorman told me a car was waiting for me at the door. When I left Washington, I had not expected to be taken out to dinner, but on the off chance that I would need it, I had packed a short dinner suit of black velvet. It was a little late in the season for velvet; but May evenings have a way of turning cool so I felt that my suit would not be out of place in case I did go out to dinner. I had let my hair down out of the tight bun I usually wore and brushed it into a pageboy style. I always felt that wearing it loose softened my features, and the black velvet brought out the highlights in my blond hair. As I left my room, I felt this would be a very exciting evening.

Sam looked resplendent in his excellently tailored dinner coat, and I was properly impressed, not only with him but also with his long black car. We went to 21 for dinner, and afterward Sam decided we should visit some gambling places. We went to places I had never heard of before.

Sam was shooting $1,000 on each roll of the dice, and he was losing. He wasn't very happy about it, and he kept trying new places. Finally, it was two in the morning, and I was worn out and ready for bed.

"How about it, Sam?" I said. "Let's call it a night. Let's let this last one really be the last."

"Oh, just one more, Cath'rine, I want to show you the biggest gambling joint in the U.S., and very hush-hush. You gotta be well known even to get in the place, much less be allowed to gamble. This place is owned by the Syndicate."

I knew I was getting in over my head. I had heard of Al Capone and the Syndicate, and I wanted no part of them. "Really, Sam, I can't go on," I pleaded. Yet the thought of the big order I had landed that afternoon kept me from putting my foot down firmly. So, against my better judgment, I gave in and we went swooshing off across the George Washington Bridge.

"Sweetheart, you won't get into any trouble, and you're so beautiful I want everyone to see the old sandhog with a real lady. You may never come my way again."

Our relationship had been strictly business, and he had not asked any questions of me, nor had I asked any of him. There was a lonesome note in his voice. I didn't know if he was married, a widower, or single. I didn't ask him if he had any children, nor had I mentioned my son, but I did notice that he seemed sad.

After about a thirty-minute ride, we arrived at what Sam referred to, with awe, as *The Club*. When the door opened, I saw what I concluded were members of the Syndicate. Never have I seen a tougher bunch of men, all dressed in white ties and tails and looking very uncomfortable.

"Oh, Sam," I remonstrated, "you know you shouldn't have brought me here!" Business or no business, deal or no deal, I knew the cost was too great. He looked at me and I saw that his armor had been pierced. There was a troubled look in his eyes. After a minute's hesitation, however, he decided to tough it out.

"Stand back, boys, stand back!" he commanded. "I'm out with a lady tonight. Stand back, I say!" And they did. They parted and Sam marched in, half dragging a reluctant me.

We went at once to the gambling room. A more beautiful room I had not seen. Here were more men in white ties and tails and women with diamonds flashing.

Sam spoke in my ear in a whisper. "See that woman over

there, the one with the diamonds everywhere she can find a place to put them?"

I nodded.

"Well, she's the moll of one of the biggest wheels in this racket. Some doll, eh?"

I looked at the hard face, pretty in a dull, stupid way, and she stared back at me until I dropped my eyes. "Sam, she must think that diamonds are a girl's best friend," I whispered.

Sam chuckled, "She no lady like you, sweetheart. You bring old Sam good luck at last."

I kept count, and when he had won $75,000, I touched his arm. "Sam, I am ill and I really must leave."

He must have believed me for he gathered up his chips and cashed them quickly. He had just taken my arm and we were preparing to leave when there was a commotion at the door. Sam grabbed me. "It's a raid!" he shouted.

Pushing through the crowd, we found a door. We rushed through it and down a flight of steps, Sam pounding along in front of me as I followed in blind panic. We reached another door and pushed it open. Standing in front of it was a cop. I dropped back, realizing the jig was up. But I had underestimated Sam. He reached into his pocket and gave the officer a handful of bills. Later he told me it was several thousand dollars. "Let us go, officer. I am with a lady from Washington."

"Very well, Mr. Rosoff," said the officer. "This way."

In a few minutes we were in the street, several blocks from The Club. Our car was nowhere in sight. Sam hailed a cab, and within forty-five minutes I was back at the Plaza.

For many years, Sam Rosoff was my good friend. The next time I saw him was at the Philadelphia convention in 1936 when Franklin D. Roosevelt was nominated for a second term of office.

As I sat in my box on the platform with my friends and family—former Governor J.C.W. Beckham, Dan Talbott, my husband, Sam Conner, and my son Jimmy—I noticed Jim Farley at the front of the platform, nodding and smiling and pointing his finger toward the back. There stood Sam Rosoff. I called him to my box and introduced him all around, saying, "This is one of the best friends I have had in my life." I never said a truer word.

Even though I no longer had an official government position, I did remain a Democratic national committeewoman through the 1930s, and people continued to call on me to use my influence in the administration. Toward the latter part of the decade, I received a phone call from Ralph McGill, editor of the *Atlanta Constitution*. He asked if I would see Mr. Walter White.

Hawk answered the door the day Mr. White came, and, seeing that he was black, instructed him to go to the back door. I scolded Hawk, telling him the man had an appointment with me. Hawk was furious. "Why didn't you tell me your appointment was a black man?"

"I don't ask people their color when they phone," I shot back.

After Mr. White and I settled in for our talk, he said that Ralph McGill told him I could point him in the direction to obtain the funding he needed. I knew immediately that we should seek Mrs. Roosevelt's help, and I proceeded to make an appointment. Mrs. Roosevelt listened carefully, then announced that she would put her full support behind the project if I would organize everything and contact various members of Congress to get their support. This I did, and we were able in 1939 to get monies for the Legal Defense Fund of the National Association for the Advancement of Colored People.

Mr. White stayed in touch for many years, keeping me advised of the progress of his organization.

All had been going well with my business, and my clients

seemed reasonably satisfied with the way I discharged my duties. I had no worries save one: Why hadn't International Aviation Corporation called me about something—anything? Since they had employed me, there had been no requests for work or information to be gathered in Washington. I felt a little nervous, but as they hadn't asked for anything, I began to neglect their affairs a bit.

Then one spring morning in 1937, I received a phone call from International Aviation, asking me if I could be in New York for a dinner meeting. All the directors from Europe and the United States were to be there; it was most important for me, their Washington representative, to attend. I, of course, said I would be there.

I was also asked to stop at the naval air station in Lakehurst, New Jersey, to pick up the president of the company, Victor Emanuel, who was returning from Europe on the famous dirigible the *Hindenburg*. I wanted to see the arrival of this magnificent ship so I got there early.

I watched as the giant dirigible hovered over the ground; when, horror of horrors, before my eyes the *Hindenburg* burst into flames. People were falling, jumping to the earth to escape the giant fireball. I screamed and screamed, Oh, those poor people! Never had I witnessed anything like the scene unfolding before me. Victor Emanuel was not among the survivors.

I drove home alone, dazed and unable to shake what I had experienced. When I arrived at my house, a telegram was waiting for me from International Aviation's office in London. I could not believe my eyes when I read it. Mr. Emanuel had been delayed. He was not a passenger on the ill-fated *Hindenburg*.

Years later, I had similar narrow escapes from death, not once but twice.

I had helped a friend, Sillman Evans, attain the presidency of the fledgling American Airlines; and in turn he said that if

I would help publicize the company by traveling on its planes, he would give me a free pass to fly anywhere the line went in the United States.

The early planes were single-motored, and I would sit up front next to the pilot. There was room for two more people in the back. We would eat our lunch from a little brown bag between stops. Most of my flights were between Louisville and Washington. We would stop in Cincinnati, Dayton, and other towns in Ohio and Pennsylvania and arrive in Washington around dark. In each town, I would disembark and exclaim to any waiting reporters how much I enjoyed the trip on American Airlines.

One day almost twenty years later, I was flying to New York from California. Sitting next to me was Jimmy Roosevelt. When we arrived in Nashville, Jimmy told me he was leaving the plane to transfer to a flight to Louisiana. Then I decided, since I was so close to Louisville, to delay my trip east and visit my parents. How close we both came to disaster! The New York flight crashed, killing all aboard.

My other brush with death came one evening when I was supposed to ride the commuter train from Washington to New York to attend an important dinner, which was scheduled at 8:30 P.M. to accommodate me because since my train wouldn't arrive until 8:00. After I'd boarded and found my seat, the conductor approached me. "Ma'am, would you mind giving this gentleman your seat?" he asked. "It is very pressing for him to get to New York on this train."

"But I need to get there, too," I replied.

"Please," the conductor pleaded. "I'll get you a seat on the next train. It's only a half hour later. Please, it's a matter of life or death for him."

Little did he know how prophetic his words were. Reluctantly, I gave the man my seat. Not long after the next train left, we passed the wreckage of the first one. Everyone on my coach had been killed.

But those near escapes were in the future. For now, the meeting with International Aviation had been rescheduled for a week and a half later, which gave me time to worry about what I might be able to contribute to it. I thought of my friend Joe Sharfsin, a lawyer and city solicitor of Philadelphia, whom I had met at the 1936 Democratic convention. He knew everything about business and politics so I phoned him about International Aviation. "Joe," I said, "if you have any thoughts on this matter, will you meet me at Thirtieth Street Station and ride up to North Station and give me some advice?"

"Of course," he answered.

I worried all the way to Philadelphia about what I would be called on to say at the meeting. I was hanging on the steps when the train pulled into Thirtieth Street Station and I saw Joe running to catch it.

When we entered the chair car, Joe wanted to know what I had been doing for International Aviation. I told him, "Nothing, absolutely nothing." They hadn't even called on me.

Joe thought a while, then said he believed they might be in difficult financial straits. Just as he spoke, the conductor came through announcing North Station. Joe jumped up to get off; as he left he called out, "I can't see anything for them to do but invoke 77-B." Then he was gone.

What in the world is 77-B, I wondered. As the train went on to New York, I wracked my brain trying to recall if I had ever heard of 77-B.

When I arrived in New York, I checked in at the Waldorf, dressed, and went down to the dinner meeting, which was held in a private dining room at the hotel. I was shaking in my boots and my hands were so cold and clammy that one of the directors commented on it.

After dinner, we went into executive meeting. I listened in amazement to the woes and troubles of International Aviation Corporation. Why, oh why, hadn't I kept closer tabs on the giant corporation?

Finally, Victor Emanuel, the president, turned to me and, smiling kindly, asked, "What has Mrs. Conner to say—or does she have any advice for us from Washington?"

I arose and, remembering Joe's last utterance, said, "Gentlemen, I have no advice to give you except that maybe 77-B is your answer."

With that, everyone let out a whoop! All began talking at once. "Wonderful, wonderful," some exclaimed. "Victor," said another, "what a wise choice you made in selecting Mrs. Conner as our Washington representative. *Of course* 77-B is our only lifeline."

As soon as the dinner was over, I rushed to my room and called Joe in Philadelphia. I told him to meet me at North Station the next morning on the early train. Again, I was hanging on the steps as the train stopped.

Joe was there, and as he followed me into my car, he was laughing. "You didn't have the glimmer of an idea what 77-B was, did you?" he asked.

"No, and I *still* don't know what it is."

"Well," he said, "you threw them into bankruptcy, that's what you did."

"No!" I was horrified. Bankruptcy had always meant ruin to me.

Joe explained that 77-B was an amendment to the Bankruptcy Act of 1898 that helped preserve a business by giving it a breathing spell to remedy its fortunes before the ax finally fell. He told me that I had actually saved the company.

I must have because relations remained excellent with them, and the company stayed my steady client until I hung up my shingle and left Washington for good.

10

A Dictator Visits Kentucky

I HAD OCCASION TO CALL on Franklin Roosevelt for help again in 1937. The weather had been dreadful in Kentucky in the early spring. It rained and rained and creeks and rivers began to overflow. One night I had a premonition that I might hear bad news; though I had been invited to dinner, I refused the invitation and remained at home alone.

When I heard the phone ring, I jumped up to answer. It was Dan Talbott calling me from Frankfort. He said that Governor Chandler was down at the old prison in a boat trying to get out the prisoners who were trapped by the rising flood, and Dan was calling on his behalf.

"For God's sake, Catherine," he cried, "try to reach Mr. Roosevelt and ask him to send some boats from New Orleans or down the Ohio. He's the only one who can help. The Coast Guard is doing what it can, but they've run out of boats."

Dan said that he had called both Kentucky senators and our representatives, but everyone was out to a party or dinner. I told him there was a reception and dinner for Kentuckians that night but that for some reason I hadn't wanted to attend. I said I would do what I could and get back to him before midnight.

I phoned Marvin McIntyre and got him at once. When I

explained the frantic appeal from Kentucky, he said, "Call the Boss. I think he and Mrs. Roosevelt are dining alone tonight."

Timidly, I called the White House number I had been given and, to my delight, got the wonderful Hackie—the telephone operator whose famous ear knew the voice of everyone who had ever called the White House. After I explained the plight of the Kentuckians in Frankfort and Louisville to her, she said she would see if she could reach the Boss. In a very few minutes she was back with Mr. Roosevelt on the phone. Again I explained the reason for my call.

"Don't worry," the president said, "I'll get the boats and I'll call both Governor Chandler and Dan Talbott tonight as soon as I can get things started."

I called Dan back to give him the heartening news. Mr. Roosevelt was as good as his word, and boats started arriving in rapid order to aid the stricken Kentucky cities.

Politics and business had given me a wide circle of friends and acquaintances. Among them was Andres Pastoriza, the Dominican Republic's charming minister to the United States.

Knowing of my close friendship with our secretary of state, Cordell Hull, Andres sought me out early in 1939 and asked if I would intercede with Mr. Hull to see that Generalissimo Rafael Leonidas Trujillo Molindas was issued an invitation to visit this country on his way to Europe later that spring. It seemed that the general, because of his reputation for undemocratic ways, was less than certain of his welcome.

I was fond of both Andres and his charming wife, Matilda, so I went to Mr. Hull the next day and told him of Andres's request. Hull sat with his feet propped up on his desk. He smiled mischievously and said that he and President Roosevelt had been discussing the general and his island only a few days before, and Andres's request fit right in with their conversation. They would be delighted to issue the general an invitation.

"Not that I approve of the way the general runs his store, young lady," Mr. Hull drawled. "But in case of war, we wouldn't want him extending his hospitality to German submarines just because we refused to extend our hospitality to him. Would we?"

The general arrived in May and was royally entertained. I met him at a dinner in his honor at the Dominican Embassy; at first, I couldn't believe all the terrible stories I had heard about him. He looked nothing like I had supposed a ruthless dictator would look—he was of medium height, stocky, with a round face, large, lively dark eyes, smooth olive complexion, a neatly trimmed mustache, iron–gray hair combed pompadour style, even white teeth, and an ever–ready smile.

Then I realized why those big dark eyes looked so lively. They were never relaxed but always on the lookout for someone. Not that they darted about, but he seemed to be able to watch everybody in a room without moving his eyeballs. And his ever–ready smile made me nervous. There was no real warmth behind it; he would turn it on and forget to turn it off, and it would dwindle down like a leaky balloon until he felt it was time to smile again—then he would pump it back up.

He had another habit that irritated me more than it made me nervous. I had heard that he spoke English perfectly; but throughout his stay, he pretended not to understand a word of it. If you spoke to him other than through Andres, he would get a faraway look in his eyes, his head would begin to turn, and invariably you would find yourself looking into his ear instead of his eyes. In short, it took me no time at all to feel completely ill at ease with the general, and I thanked my stars that it was Andres's job to entertain him, not mine.

So what happened after dinner? Here came Andres. "Cath'rine, again I have the small favor to ask," he said, his accent dripping charm. "My general desires to improve the breeding of our horses. He wants to buy horses here, and your state of Kentucky is the horse country. I wish very much you might ask him to visit you and show to him the stock farms and your so beautiful state. Will it be asking too much of you, Cath'rine?"

Immediately, small unpatriotic voices within me began warning against it. If I felt ill at ease with the general in Washington, D.C., I would have a nervous breakdown if he were at my house in Bardstown, Kentucky. But then I thought of German submarines, and I knew Mr. Hull would smile and say: "We invited him for you, young lady. *You* entertain him."

With a sigh and a brave smile, I told Andres that I would be delighted to have the general visit me in Bardstown and to tour the horse farms in the Bluegrass. When would the general like to come? Andres looked as though he hated to disappoint me. The general, he said, would not be able to visit Kentucky until October, on his way home from Europe.

What a relief that was. At least I would have five months to prepare for his visit. To make certain that nothing would occur to make him change his mind about the German submarines, I began the very next day calling my friends in Kentucky. Well before October, everything had been arranged. Mr. Hull and the State Department were most happy.

It was to be a three–day visit. I understood that the general, Andres, and an aide would visit. I would precede them to Kentucky; with Mildred Chandler, representing Governor Happy Chandler, we would meet them when they arrived by train in Louisville. We would then motor to Lexington for a luncheon at the beautiful farm home of Frazer Lebus, prominent horseman and tobacco grower and a mutual friend of Mr. Hull's and mine.

After the luncheon, we would visit the famous horse Man O' War and Colonel E.R. Bradley's Idle Hour Stock Farm and then go to Keeneland Race Course, which was having its fall meet. Following the races, there would be dinner at the Governor's Mansion in Frankfort, and then we would go to my home in Bardstown. Using it as a base of operations, we would spend the rest of the general's stay visiting other horse farms in the Bluegrass.

The only hint of the disaster that lay ahead came when I dropped by to see Mr. Hull before departing for Kentucky. He was pleased to hear that everything was all set, and he was also amused. "Young lady," he said, peering at me over his glasses and smiling, "I think your friend Andres is a little worried. He's been hearing that Kentucky is famous not only for its horses and women but also for its feuding. He doesn't want his general caught in any cross fire." What a big laugh Mr. Hull and I had over that.

Saturday morning, October 22, at nine o'clock, Mildred and I were at the Chesapeake and Ohio station in Louisville awaiting our general. With us were the drivers of the two Cadillacs I had arranged for, reporters, photographers, a motorcycle policeman to escort us, and about a hundred onlookers waiting to see their first live dictator.

I should have been nervous, but I was too busy trying to convince Mildred there was nothing to be nervous about. Representing Happy, who had an engagement in Chicago, she felt as responsible for the success of the expedition as I did.

"Mildred, there will only be the general, Andres, and an aide," I said. "We'll go to Lexington, come back for dinner at the mansion, and then I will take them to Bardstown and your responsibilities will be over. Now, relax."

The train pulled in at 9:30 A.M. I saw Andres walking briskly to meet us, smiling as usual. "Oh, there's Andres!" I said excitedly.

"But what's that behind him?" Mildred asked, sounding more frightened than excited.

In Andres's wake was a veritable crowd of men; in the middle was the general.

Mildred sensed my dismay. "How many did you say were coming?" she asked.

"They're probably just reporters," I said while hurrying toward Andres. I wanted a few words in private with him before his entourage caught up.

"Ah, Cath'rine," he said, taking my hand, "the general, he thinks your Kentucky is so beautiful."

"Never mind that," I snapped. "Who are all these people?"

"Only a few members of the embassy staff," he answered, pretending not to notice the frantic look on my face. "The general thought they would like to see your beautiful Kentucky, also."

Embassy staff, my foot, I thought, glancing wildly over his shoulder at the approaching mob. Two or three of the men were in uniform and might be military aides, and a couple looked like secretaries; but the rest—all big, swarthy, sinister-looking men—were definitely bodyguards. Mr. Hull hadn't been joking when he said that Andres and the general were worried about my beautiful Kentucky's reputation for gunplay.

"But Andres, I arranged for only two cars," I whispered desperately. "I'll have to arrange for a whole fleet now."

"Do so, please," he said, still smiling. "The general he does not like to be kept waiting."

I started to snap back that I did not like to have fourteen people show up when I was expecting only three. But I controlled myself and introduced him to Mildred. Then the phalanx opened up and we greeted the general. He was wearing a double–breasted gray suit, a striped shirt, a big flowery tie, and his mechanical smile. His eyes were already searching the crowd for any sign of squirrel rifles.

While Mildred fervently told him how sorry she was that Happy couldn't be there in person, I excused myself and went into the station to call the Cadillac agency to ask for more cars. There were no more Cadillacs for hire, but they would arrange to send three Ford trucks.

Then I called Frazer Lebus in Lexington. He was expecting only five of us for lunch. "Frazer," I wailed, "he's brought his whole army with him."

Angel that he was, Frazer only laughed. "We'll set up a field kitchen. Bring them on."

Feeling a little less like jumping in the river, I returned to my safari and found the general ignoring the questions of the reporters in favor of smiling at the crowd—only he really wasn't smiling. Along with his circle of bodyguards, he was still casing the crowd for guns.

One of the reporters, tired of being ignored, turned to me to confirm the general's itinerary. "Mrs. Conner," he asked wearily, "the general and his staff will be staying at your home in Bardstown during their visit—is that right?"

Mildred and I rolled our eyes at each other and inwardly began counting my bedrooms in Bardstown. The house was big, but it was not a dormitory. The general's "staff" was about to become the first ever to bivouac on a roof. I must have looked as though I was about to panic, because Mildred gave a long, drawn-out sigh, turned to the reporter, and said, "No, the general and his staff will be staying at the Governor's Mansion—at least for tonight."

At that moment I was so relieved that I was fool enough to think my troubles were over. We chatted for a few more minutes while the photographers took pictures, and then here came the Ford trucks. Mildred, the general, Andres, and I got into the first Cadillac, then the men in uniform and a secretary or two got into the second one, and the bodyguards piled into the trucks.

At last we were ready to go, I thought. I told the chauffeur to inform the motorcycle policeman in front of us that he could proceed; but at that same moment, the general leaned forward and said something in rapid Spanish to Andres, who restrained the chauffeur and turned to me. "Cath'rine, the general he is not happy with the one policeman. He would like to have more."

Suddenly, I didn't care whether the general understood English or not. "What in the world for?" I snapped. "He's got his army." I groaned and yelled for the chauffeur to tell the policeman to slow down and stop blowing his silly siren so loudly. The chauffeur began blowing his horn to attract the attention of the policeman, who, thinking it was a signal for more speed, began blaring the siren even louder and going faster.

We followed him to the county line, where two state troopers, upon sighting us, evidently thought that speed and noise were the order of the day. So they swung out in front of us, took over the lead, and we roared to Lexington.

The next ten hours were a blur. I'm sure the general enjoyed the lovely luncheon at Frazer's home and seeing Man O' War and Idle Hour Farm and the races at Keeneland, but it was all lost on me. I had the feeling that it was the lull before the storm and that with the coming of night, the general and his little chums would start acting up again.

Sure enough, as soon as we returned to Frankfort and poor Mildred welcomed the general to the mansion, things started building to a gruesome climax.

First, one of Mildred's dear friends "accidentally" dropped in—she claimed she had no idea we were entertaining such distinguished guests—and before leaving, she laughingly told Andres that she supposed the general knew that all the servants in the mansion were convicted murderers recruited from the state penitentiary.

This was true—but none of them had committed more than one murder; except for that one slip, they were all of good character and very trustworthy. Mildred and I did our best to explain this to Andres and the general but to no avail. The result was like spending an evening with a bunch of whirling dervishes. Every time one of the servants entered the room, the general's bodyguards would follow his every move until he left the room.

And the servants were just as trusting of the bodyguards. "They the meanest lookin' guests evah been here," I overheard one of them say when I took a trip back to the kitchen. "If they's all like that, I don't never want to go to no Domino Republic."

It was in this atmosphere that Mildred and I spent the evening trying to entertain our guests. Finally, around eleven o'clock, the general, through Andres, announced that he would like to retire. Poor Andres, who, because of his duties as interpreter, had to do twice as much talking as everyone else, looked as relieved as we did.

But no relief was to be had. There were eight bedrooms in the mansion—six on the second floor and two on the third. After assigning our guests to their rooms, Mildred and I were left with the smallest bedroom on the third floor, one containing a narrow single bed that looked hardly large enough for a child, much less two exhausted women who wanted to spread out and collapse.

At two in the morning we were still awake—partly because there was absolutely no way for the two of us to get comfortable and partly because Mildred couldn't forget her lovely guests downstairs. She had bolstered the general's staff by calling in several capitol guards, but she was still worried about something happening and throwing the general into a turmoil.

"Catherine," she mourned, "with hundreds of kings and presidents in this world, why did you have to bring me a dictator? And a gun–shy one, at that."

"Just try to think of the German submarines," I pleaded.

At 2:30 A.M. the curtain went up on the final act. Mildred and I were still awake but not talking, both occupied with our miserable little thoughts of what horrors the morning would bring.

Suddenly Mildred nudged me. "Catherine, do you hear that?"

I cringed and listened. Somewhere out in front of the mansion a horn was blowing. "It's just a car horn," I said.

She started to get out of the bed. "*Just* a car horn? It could be a signal. Maybe somebody *is* after the general. Maybe his enemies did hire some assassins around here and that's the signal for them to rise up."

I sat upright in the bed and told her to stop it, that she was being sillier than the general. She ignored me and started putting on her robe. "If that man is killed here, you know who the Republicans will blame it on—Happy!" She started for the door.

The horn kept blowing.

"Wait for me," I said as I got up and put on my robe. We started easing down the stairs. Should we awaken Trujillo's guards? We both voted no. If it were a false alarm, it would still take the rest of the night for us to quiet them down. First, we would check on the general and Andres in the governor's suite to see if they were all right.

At the foot of the stairs, we turned and silently made our way to the alcove leading to the governor's suite. Suddenly, Mildred, who was leading the way, stumbled in the dark. "Good lord!" she gasped. "It's a body!"

I thought I was going to faint. Had the assassins already been at work? I could see the entire population of the Dominican Republic lining the island's shores to welcome German submarines. Then we heard the body snoring, then another body snoring, and another. The guards weren't in their rooms; they were sleeping on the floor in front of the general's door!

"For heaven's sake," I pleaded, "please don't step on them."

"Stop talking so loud," Mildred admonished as one of the general's men stirred, "and come on."

Sidestepping sleeping bodies, we made it to the front door. I went out last; as I did, I heard a gabble of Spanish behind me. One or some of the general's retinue had awakened. Out on the porch, I started to report this fact to Mildred but was distracted by something that seemed at least as important. "Mildred!" I called as loudly as I dared, "we're barefooted. Can't we just send the mansion guard out?"

There was no answer. She was already down the steps and headed across the lawn toward the horn blower. I took it for granted that she was more mad than scared now and didn't even realize that she was barefooted—or that we were out at 3:00 A.M. in nothing but our nightgowns and robes.

I fell in behind her and on we marched. When we were halfway across the lawn, I realized that there was something strange about our formation. The guard should be leading the procession, not us. I turned around, and there he was directly behind me, pistol in hand.

"Mildred," I pleaded, "will you please put your policeman in front, or at least have him take his gun out of my back?"

By the time he had taken his place at the head of our posse, we had reached the car. It was parked under a streetlight and the horn was still blowing. Behind the wheel was a young man so drunk that he evidently thought he was in front of his girl's house or else a curb–service tavern. Even after seeing us approach, he continued to blow the horn.

Mildred, realizing he wasn't an assassin, became even more furious. "Are you trying to get shot?" she hollered in the car window at him. "Stop blowing that horn and get out of here."

He wasn't the least bit impressed. He leaned across the front seat and glared at Mildred. "Who the hell do you think you are, giving me orders?" he demanded drunkenly.

That made *me* furious. "She's the governor's wife, that's who she is!" I snapped.

"Governor's wife?" he laughed. "Out in her nightgown? You're just a couple of old bats."

Then Mildred exploded. Drawing herself up to her full

five feet five, she thrust her finger at the man and screamed at the guard, "Arrest that man!"

Up to that point, the guard had been standing by admiring the moon and trying to pretend that he wasn't part of the scene. Or maybe he was so sleepy that he thought the whole thing was a nightmare. But Mildred's imperious command snapped him out of his coma. He ran around the car, snatched the man out, shoved his gun into the small of the man's back, and we began the march back to the mansion.

We were halfway there before our prisoner recovered his speech and began babbling his apologies and asking how he was supposed to recognize a governor's wife walking around barefooted and in a nightgown at three in the morning.

Our guard tried to make up for his previous lack of indignation on our behalf. "Well, she *is* the governor's wife," he said, "and she's entertaining a general, and his whole army is ready to machine gun you down. If you don't shut your mouth about nightgowns I'm gonna let 'em."

It was a pretty speech, but we were more worried than warmed by it. Were the bodyguards awake? We glanced up at the mansion windows and breathed a sigh of relief. Not a light was showing.

"We'll go around back," Mildred whispered, "so we don't wake them up. Keep him outside and I'll go in and phone the police."

"There's really people in there with machine guns?" our prisoner whispered anxiously to the guard.

"They got 'em," the guard replied, "and they don't talk no American, so they ain't no use in you pleadin' with 'em."

Mildred and I couldn't help snickering, but what a mistake that was. Reaching the back of the mansion, Mildred went up the steps, opened the door, and there, silhouetted in the dim light from the hall, were two of the biggest bodyguards. There was no mistaking what they had in their hands—submachine guns.

It was too much for our prisoner. One look and he jerked away from the guard and raced across the garden.

Immediately, the mansion guard bellowed, "Come back here or I'll . . ."

"Don't shoot!" Mildred screamed, racing back down the steps. She was too late. The guard fired over the fugitive's head. That was all it took. Overhead, all hell suddenly broke loose. The bodyguards were blasting away from the windows on the garden side. They had been awake all the time watching us bring the "assassin" in.

For a second Mildred and I were too petrified to move. Then, nightgowns flying, we raced around the side of the mansion, screaming, "Don't kill him! He's just a drunk! Don't kill him! Stop that idiotic shooting!"

In the moonlight, we saw our former prisoner make one magnificent leap, soar over the garden wall, and disappear. The firing stopped.

Without a word to each other, Mildred and I stumbled around to the front steps and hobbled into the mansion. There, standing on the stairs, fully clothed and ready to flee, were Andres and the general. Andres was staring wildly at us. The general, a more practical man, was starting toward the windows, as though he was trying to decide which one he was going out.

How long we tried to explain to them that it wasn't an assassination attempt I don't know. The next thing I knew it was 5:00 A.M., Mildred and I were on our bed of pain, and a servant was knocking at the door.

"Miz Chandler," he called out softly, "you know that gentleman in the governor's room? Well, he done rung his bell; and when I went up there he's all dressed and sittin' in a chair with a big gun in his lap. I'se scared to go back."

"Well, what does he want?" Mildred asked pitifully.

"That's another thing, Miz Chandler. I can't understand a thing he say, but from the way he say it, I think he wanna leave."

Sure enough, that afternoon, with reporters still trying to find out *why* he was leaving, the general departed for Washington. The next day, the Associated Press story in the *Louisville Courier–Journal* was headlined: "Trujillo Cuts Short Kentucky Visit, Leaves for Washington Two Days Early."

To give the devil his due, I must add that the general gave no haven to German submarines during the war; and immediately upon his return home, he sent me a signed photograph of himself, thanking me for being, of all things, a perfect hostess. Later, when I visited the Dominican Republic on a Caribbean cruise, he insisted on giving a party for me at his home—where I noticed that those dark eyes, even there, searched the rooms for the presence of death.

11

Cultural Exchanges

ONE DAY IN THE SPRING of 1939, I went to Philadelphia to attend a concert conducted by Leopold Stokowski. My friend Joe Sharfsin was going to be my escort. As Hawk drove me to the railway station, we passed the basin where the cherry trees were in riotous bloom. A few years later, when we were fighting Japan, I could never see those beautiful trees blooming without an ache in my heart for all of us who had enjoyed this gift from the Japanese and now were at war with them.

That night, Stokowski stood on the stage and described our continent, "lying carved so beautifully between the Atlantic and Pacific oceans," and he pleaded for stronger ties of friendship. An idea began forming in my mind. I leaned over to Joe and whispered, "May I meet the maestro after the concert?"

"Certainly," he quickly answered. "'Stoky' is my best friend. I'll take you backstage."

It was a very successful meeting. The maestro was in full agreement with the plan I outlined to him that night, which was a simple one. I would undertake to get the State Department to sponsor and pay expenses for an orchestra of young American musicians to be sent on a tour of South America, with the maestro as conductor; a similar tour would be arranged in South America to return the visit the following year.

We talked enthusiastically all night; when we left Stokowski's apartment in the concert hall the next morning at seven, still dressed in our evening clothes, many curious glances were cast our way, especially by the clerk at my hotel.

I returned to Washington on the first train I could get and hurried straight to the State Department and to my friend Cordell Hull, the secretary of state. Mr. Hull, who was very interested in forming closer ties with our neighbors to the south, thought it was a great idea; but he said he needed some time to think it over. First, he had to consult President Roosevelt. He suggested that perhaps the National Youth Administration might be the agency to sponsor such a project.

I hurried home and called Stokowski. We were both jubilant.

It was two weeks before I heard from Secretary Hull. Then one morning the phone rang and Mr. Hull said, "The Boss thinks you have hit on a great idea, and he is going to give it his full support."

As the idea progressed toward realization, it grew bigger and bigger until we realized that the National Youth Administration would need extra funding for such a project. Its chairman, Aubrey Williams, was concerned about the mode of travel. He could not find a ship that was in condition to take the group. To purchase a ship, or even lease one, was out of the question.

I offered to try to get a ship, and I did! My friend William Franklin, owner of the Franklin Steamship Lines of New York and Philadelphia, let us use one.

Our executive committee was composed of Aubrey Williams; Leo S. Rowe, director general of the Pan American Union; Colby Chester, president of General Foods; T.H. McInnerney, president of National Dairy Products; William S. Paley, president of the Columbia Broadcasting System; Joe Sharfsin as legal counsel; and me. We decided that we needed some real publicity behind our project because we were going to have to ask Congress for an additional loan to the National Youth Administration.

The plan was simple. We needed social recognition to arouse the curiosity and interest of the public, and I was selected to give a party that would include the ambassadors and their wives of the twenty-one countries of South America who might conceivably be interested in the project. It was agreed that I would host a supper for the ambassadors and their wives to meet Stokowski after a concert he would give in Washington.

As an encore following the performance, he announced the "Liebestod" from *Tristan und Isolde*—"for a very dear friend," he said, with a glance at my box. I was very moved by the recognition.

When I told Hawk that I was going to give the most important party of my life for a man named Stokowski, he jumped at me, pointing his finger at my nose. "Him? Why, I knows him—well, not to say him personally—but I knows his position in life. He's a big music man." From that time on, it was Hawk's party. He was beside himself.

My house looked particularly beautiful the night of the party. Hawk had done it in white and lavender lilacs. The great bowls of the fluffy, fragrant spring flowers, together with all the candles lit in the candelabras, gave my old house in Georgetown a fairy-tale look.

Supper was served at midnight. Hawk, in his swallowtail coat and flowing tie, was at the door with his widest smile. Stokowski arrived last. His entrance was so perfectly timed that I wondered if it had been planned that way.

All of my guests were interested in our project. They gathered in groups; under the wise guidance of Rowe, of the Pan American Union, they offered many valid suggestions to Secretary Hull, Aubrey Williams, Stokowski, and me.

The party drew to a close as the candles slowly died. The drawing room had taken on the air of a softly fading night. It was 4:15 A.M. Guests were beginning to stir in anticipation of leaving, and the maestro yawned. Secretary Hull, Aubrey Williams, and others had already gone, and those remaining were having a nightcap, when Hawk floated in.

"Maestro," he said, "I's been looking forward to this meeting all my life, I guess."

Stokowski looked up with a flicker of interest in his eyes. Later I was to learn that he was always on the lookout for talent, pursuing it with the directness of a hunter stalking a deer. "Why does this meeting mean so much to you?" he inquired in his beautifully modulated voice.

"Because," Hawk continued, "in my small way, I composes, too."

"You do?" The maestro was definitely intrigued, and I knew I didn't have a chance to stop Hawk so I had to trust that "Stoky" would be gentle with him.

"Yes, sir," Hawk reiterated, "I's a composer."

Stokowski took one long look and perhaps thought it the better part of wisdom not to continue, for I saw a small frown appear on his brow. Nevertheless, he plunged. "Well, tell me now—what have you composed?"

The guests froze, as did I—but not Hawk. He squared himself and let forth with the first lines of his composition: "The Same Dog That Bit You, Hot Mama, She Done Snapped at Me Too." He gave it everything he had—all five stanzas of it.

When he finished, there was dead silence. Hawk stared in disbelief. Always before, everyone had applauded like mad when he sang.

Finally, Stoky let forth with a howl of mirth that shook the neighborhood. "Hawk, that was wonderful," he laughed. "In these troubled times perhaps we should have more of your kind of music; it's so good to laugh."

Still laughing, Stokowski bade us all good night and shook Hawk's hand. "Again, thank you, Hawk," he said.

As the famous conductor walked off into the morning, Hawk whispered to me, "He is a real gentleman, Ole Miss."

The party was declared a great success by the social press of Washington, and it gained wide publicity for the tour. Even Congress, apparently, had been impressed, for the necessary money was appropriated. The tour of the American Youth Orchestra took place in July and August 1940, visiting around a dozen cities, including Havana, Montevideo, Buenos Aires, and Rio de Janeiro. It was the first official cultural exchange the United States had ever undertaken.

My next adventure with My Old Kentucky Home came in this same period. Jim Farley called me one afternoon in his capacity as postmaster general to tell me a stamp was being issued to commemorate Stephen Foster and that the state of Florida was pushing him to issue it for "Swanee River" because the Suwannee River the song was named for is located in that state.

"But Jim," I protested, "My Old Kentucky Home is the proper place for that first stamp sale. The word 'home' means something to every living soul, while 'Swanee River' is just a melody to sing."

My persuasion prevailed, and the first-day sale of the stamp was set for May 3, 1940, at Bardstown. Bing Crosby would sing "My Old Kentucky Home" on a radio broadcast from California with Stokowski directing the orchestra.

At about the same time, I received a phone call from Colonel Matt Winn, president of Churchill Downs. That great promoter of the Kentucky Derby was trying to revitalize the race because Prohibition and the Depression had made serious inroads on the historic track's popularity. So he called me in Washington and asked me if I could get some celebrities to come to the 1940 Derby for publicity's sake.

I told him I was giving a big party the day before for Postmaster General Jim Farley for the first-day sale of the Stephen

Foster stamp and that I would get all my guests to stay on for the Derby. He was delighted with my guest list and offered to furnish box seats for them all if I would pay for their luncheon.

Many of the people involved with the American Youth Orchestra came by private Pullman from New York, including T.H. McInnerney, Colby Chester, William Franklin, and Jim Bruce, vice-president of National Dairy Products. From Washington came my former boss Harry Hopkins and Hugh Johnson, head of the National Recovery Administration. Among the Californians who came were Kentucky-born actress Irene Dunne and her husband; character actor Walter Connolly and his wife, actress Nedda Harrigan; and Bill Quigley, president of the Del Mar Race Track. Other guests included artist Howard Chandler Christy; heavyweight boxing champion Jack Dempsey; Jack Kelly of Philadelphia, whose sister Grace became first a movie star and then a princess; plus the governor of Tennessee, the minister to Canada, and the ambassador from the Philippines—some ninety guests in all.

I had buses—and policemen galore—ready to take them to Bardstown for the unveiling of the stamp. Then we returned to Louisville for dinner in the Rathskeller of the Seelbach Hotel, where I had taken over the third floor to house them all. The next morning I gave a reception at the hotel for Jim Farley, after which we were off to the track. Many of the guests had never attended a Derby and were full of great expectations.

My luncheon was held in a private dining room at Churchill Downs. New York columnist Inez Robb did a radio broadcast live from the room. The menu included shrimp, fillet of beef, and the Kentucky specialties of fried chicken, corn pudding, green beans, and a bibb lettuce salad. For dessert there was green mint ice and apple pie a la mode. The drinks were iced tea, coffee, champagne, and, of course, mint juleps.

I had ordered the waiters to serve one mint julep to each

guest. They were made, by special order, from my father's old recipe, and strong. I knew the juleps' potency; but most of my guests were unfamiliar with them, and they ordered them again and again. As they drank, they gathered in groups and told stories, and the juleps continued to flow.

They never saw a race. They stayed in the dining room until late afternoon when the band began to play "My Old Kentucky Home" before the Derby, and then they all wept together.

It must have been the most confused group of guests ever to have gathered at Churchill Downs. They lost their coats, hats, wallets, bet tickets on the Derby, plane tickets—everything that was loose on their bodies.

Neville Miller, who was the former mayor of Louisville and one of my guests, called the police for help. With the waiters and policemen, the ex-mayor and I finally got some order out of the chaos. By nine that night, I had placed my guests back in their private train cars and gotten planes to wait for missing passengers. Finally, the last one, Harry Hopkins, had been put on a train for New Orleans with the promise that we would send him his missing overcoat as soon as we found it.

Late that night, a few guests who were staying on with me until Sunday arrived with me back at my home in Bardstown. It was a weary group I saw off the next day. The one thing that remained indelibly printed on my mind was that I had not changed hat or dress from Thursday to Sunday. I had merely washed my face and hands, put on lipstick, and brushed my hair. What a weekend!

The press duly reported my Derby party, to the delight of Colonel Winn. He was so pleased he gave me my own lifetime box at Churchill Downs.

12

Major Changes

LATE IN 1939, Hawk was driving me to Florida to visit a friend when we had a frightening experience. We were traveling through Georgia; and for an hour it seemed we had been following a farmer who was herding his stock down the middle of the road. I had become very impatient by the time we crept into a little town. "Blow the horn!" I commanded Hawk, and he proceeded to do so.

Immediately, from the porch of a little country store stepped a burly white man in overalls. He came around to Hawk's window. "We don't let no goddamn niggers blow their horns in this town, boy," he scowled.

Evidently, he had not seen me in the back seat. I opened the door and stepped out. "Do you allow me to blow the horn?" I asked.

"Well . . . well, yes, ma'am," he stammered.

"I told him to do it, and he did," I shot back. "Where's the nearest phone?"

I marched into the grocery and dialed directly through to the governor of Georgia's office. (Governor Eurith D. Rivers had been to parties at my house on several occasions.)

"Catherine," he apologized, "I'm so sorry. I'll be there within the hour. If I can't get away, I'll send some state troopers."

Forty-five minutes later, two of the biggest troopers I had ever seen pulled up and proceeded to rake our antagonist over the coals. Then they provided Hawk and me with our own personal escort to the Florida state line.

While I was in Florida I first heard talk of a third term for President Roosevelt. A Washington-based reporter spotted me on the beach at Palm Beach and asked me how I felt about a third term. I was astonished. I called all my closest advisers, Jim Farley, Senator Byrd, Vice-President Garner, and Dan Talbott. They all said they felt that it was a mistake but that he could be reelected.

I caught the first available flight to Washington, and when I got home, I found a note from Marvin McIntyre asking me to call him.

"Where have you been?" he asked. "I've been trying to reach you. The Boss is wild. He's questioning everyone on the National Committee to see who's going to support him."

"What are they saying?"

"Some are for him and some are against him."

"Mac, I'll have to say I'm against him. I can't be for a third term."

I had been the staunchest supporter of President Roosevelt. For eight years I had watched in wonder and amazement as that great brain gave itself to shaping the United States for the task of becoming a world power. Then some things began to happen that I couldn't understand.

President Roosevelt wanted to change the Supreme Court from nine to fifteen members. The nine were a very conservative group so he wanted to appoint some justices who were liberal—extremely liberal. Adolph Hitler was doing something similar in Germany, using the courts to justify his actions. I had gone to my friends in the Congress, both the House and the Senate, and found everyone discussing the Supreme Court. All the issues that had been turned down by the original nine members were being brought up again. Of course, if there were new appointees, they would swing the Court to the president's side.

That aside, I could not support a third term for anyone, feeling that it was the intention of the Founding Fathers to limit the presidency to two terms. Then, too, you could just look at the president and see how ill he was, worn to a frazzle.

I made an appointment to see him; when I entered the Oval Office, he was busy signing papers and left me standing in an awkward silence. Finally, he pushed the papers away, took a cigarette out of my pink jade box, stuck it into his holder, and lit it.

"Be seated, Catherine," he said. "How are you after your trip to Florida?" He went on to say that most of the important Democrats and some Republicans were urging him to run for a third term and added that he felt the war in Europe demanded his presence at the helm of state. Then he asked me how I felt.

A cold sweat broke over my whole body. I couldn't speak. I could only stare at him. We looked at each other. Finally, I stood up.

"Mr. Roosevelt," I said, "I cannot support you for a third term."

He pushed the jade cigarette box toward me. I remembered what he had said when I gave it to him.

"Is this the end of our friendship?" I asked.

"I'm afraid so," he replied.

I picked up the box and turned to go. "Good-bye, Mr. President."

His answer was cold. "Good-bye, Mrs. Conner."

In July 1940, I was reelected as national Democratic committeewoman, but I could feel that a chapter in my life was ending. In October, I filed suit for a divorce from Sam Conner. For years, ours had been a marriage in name only because our lives had taken such different directions. It was an amicable divorce.

I also closed my public relations business in Washington. After a brief winter visit in Florida, I married T.H. McInnerney, president of National Dairy Products Corporation, in Palm Beach. I am not sure why I did this, but from the beginning it was clear that it was a mistake.

The day we were married, I had one of my periodic spells of sinus trouble. I never knew what caused those dreadful attacks—perhaps nerves, perhaps emotions, or maybe just a virus. But I became very ill and was unable to return to New York with my new husband. I stayed in Florida a few days longer and sent Hawk, my maid Julia, and my car back to Kentucky—the car for my son Jimmy when he was home for vacations from the University of Virginia.

I arrived in New York to join McInnerney on a gloomy, snowy, cold February afternoon. That very night I realized that, though my new husband had a cook, a butler, and two maids, not one of them had been properly trained. My first dinner at 820 Fifth Avenue consisted of a strained vegetable soup, dry ham and fried potatoes, a lettuce salad, and fruit jello for dessert. I wondered how he could know so little about good food and service. I ate practically nothing, and, pleading my illness, retired as soon as possible to my own quarters.

Upon awakening the next morning, I rang my bell for breakfast. The woman who was to be my own personal maid answered and brought me a delightful breakfast. So I learned that Anna, the cook, really did know her business. She and I became fast friends and remained so until I departed. Under my direction, she turned out some delectable meals.

Before we were married, McInnerney had visited me twice in Kentucky and several times in Washington and had always bragged about my luncheons and dinners. I think he married me because he thought I was a great hostess. He wanted a hostess—he didn't want me. I felt as though he'd hired me.

He had also lied to me about his age. He'd said he was sixty.
I learned he was seventy-three.

As the wife of an enormously wealthy corporation president, I was to see more bankers, industrialists, and conservative millionaires than in my days in Democratic politics. But
not long after my arrival in New York, I was returning to our
apartment when I saw my great hero of 1928—Al Smith was
just ahead of me.

"Governor," I called.

He turned and, seeing me, gave that famous grin of his.
"Why, what are you doing in New York?" he asked.

I told him of my marriage, and we discovered that he lived
on the seventh floor and I on the eighth of the same building.
When we reached his floor, he insisted that I visit with him for
an hour or so. That began a series of afternoons that were
pure pleasure and made life bearable for me.

Mrs. Smith, who didn't like alcohol, was most tolerant of
Governor Smith and my enjoying his famous old-fashioneds.
Sometimes Jim Farley would join us to exchange stories about
our golden years in politics. Governor Smith always laughed
about the time he was making a speech in Louisville in late
July. I had headed my county's march from the Ballard Mill
on Broadway to the Armory, some fifteen blocks away, where
Smith was to make his speech. The sun blazed, the streets
seethed, the loyal followers sweated and endured. When we
reached the Armory, the dear Republicans had gotten to the
building's heating system and turned it on full blast! The place
was a living hell. But the governor was at his best, as he always was when the going got rough.

These visits were greatly resented by McInnerney, who
hated the Democratic party and Roosevelt. I soon found that
I had closed not only my public relations business but every
opening I had to peace of mind, happiness, and joy of living.
To my horror, I found that I had promised to obey, to honor—
and in so doing had sold my body to—an iceberg who called

himself a man. Such conceit as he revealed little by little I had never known.

The weeks dragged on, relieved only by my visits with Governor Smith. Then one day in late March, I met two charming people, Mr. and Mrs. Jeremiah (Jerry) Milband of New York and Connecticut. Through them, I met the former president of the United States, Herbert Hoover. At the Milband home in Greenwich, Connecticut, I had the honor of being seated by the side of Mr. Hoover. I forged a lasting friendship with him. I found him to be one of the truly great Americans. Even McInnerney approved!

It was through President Hoover that I met Dr. Nicholas Murray Butler. He was the president of Columbia University and a brilliant man who sought the ideal solution of peace through education. To me, listening to Hoover and Butler exchange ideas was an education. It was through them that I learned to respect the Republican party with its many brilliant leaders.

When we received an invitation to attend a dinner given by Butler and his wife, I knew the evening held promise of great enjoyment. What I didn't know was the wonderful surprise it held for me.

I don't recall all of the guests who were there, but I remember President Hoover and also the man who was president of the *London Times,* who was extremely pro-British in his remarks about New York and very enthusiastic about the restoration of Williamsburg, Virginia. I, too, thought the restoration of Williamsburg a wonderful project; but his disparagement of the United States and his raving about Williamsburg had even the mild-mannered President Hoover glancing around with that hurt look he sometimes wore when he thought a remark was ungracious or out of line.

The one person who proved a surprise for me, however, was a Mr. Johnson who accompanied me in to dinner. As we sat talking through the first course, he kept looking at me so intently that I became very self-conscious. Finally, he asked, "Mrs. McInnerney, what part of the country are you from?" "Kentucky," I replied.

"What part of Kentucky?" he continued.

"Originally from Bullitt County, but in 1920 I moved to the small town of Bardstown, in Nelson County." Thinking he wouldn't know the town, I hastened to add that it was the location of My Old Kentucky Home.

Mr. Johnson squared himself and looked at me intently. "You wouldn't have ever heard of Jim Rouse, would you?" he asked.

My heart almost stopped beating. "He's my father," I replied.

"Well, I'm from Lebanon, Kentucky," Mr. Johnson continued, "and your father and I once had rival baseball teams. My, we fought. You call him tomorrow and get him up here. I want to talk over old times with him."

On the way home that night, McInnerney wanted to know what Percy Johnson and I had talked about. My father, I told him, and explained that Mr. Johnson wanted me to have him up for a visit so they could have some talks about long ago. This gave McInnerney a jolt because he was trying to get a loan for several millions from the Chemical Bank, of which Mr. Johnson was president. He suggested I call my father and ask him to call Mr. Johnson and put in a word for him.

The next morning I did call my father to tell him about my meeting with Percy Johnson, and I also gave him McInnerney's message. Papa said he would make the call, which he did. Mr. Johnson phoned me the next day to tell me that he and my father had talked for over an hour. McInnerney often made fun of my Kentucky heritage, but he certainly could use my relatives when he thought it would be to his benefit.

One night as we sat in front of the fire, McInnerney said he would like to give a dinner, returning the Butlers' and Milbands' hospitality. He wanted to invite Eddie Johnson, manager of the Metropolitan Opera, Percy Johnson, and the popular basso Ezio Pinza.

It was a delightful dinner. Our dining room, which could seat seventy-five people, was reduced in size for a small party and decorated like a flower garden. McInnerney really beamed. He was on the board of the Metropolitan Opera, which he felt gave him a very important position in New York society. Because of his position, I was asked to be a member of the Metropolitan Opera Guild, which was chaired by Mrs. August Belmont. She was a beautiful woman but one I felt I could never be close to.

The final blow to my marriage with McInnerney came one night at another dinner party. During dinner, the butler came in and told me that my son was in the hall, very nervous and wanting to see me right away. McInnerney overheard the butler telling me that Jimmy was joining the air corps.

"That's just where that so-and-so ought to be," he sneered.

"How dare you!" I shot back. That was the last straw. I got up and left the table, and I was gone by the next morning.

Jimmy went back home to tell my parents he was joining the air corps. While he was there, he caught up on a lot of work around the house in Bardstown, which I had given him and his father when we divorced. We surmised that he was very tired when he left that evening to take his dinner date back to Louisville. We believe he fell asleep at the wheel. He had a terrible accident. The young woman was not severely injured, but Jimmy was thrown from the car and his face hit a post beside the highway. A family friend happened to be driving behind Jimmy's car and saw the whole thing.

My son was rushed to Norton Hospital in Louisville, where he was cared for by the same doctor who took care of General George Patton when he had his accident. Jimmy was in a coma for three months, and I remained at his side. I don't know what I would have done without the help of Sam Conner and my mother and father.

Then one day, as I sat staring at Jimmy, he opened his eyes and said, "Hi, Mother." It was the happiest day of my life. A week later, I took him home to Bardstown. Sam wanted me to come home, too, and I was giving a lot of thought to reconciliation.

But there were more problems with Jimmy. His teeth were in such a terrible condition from the wreck that he needed special attention. My friend Harry Goetz, who had been a client, telephoned with a suggestion. Harry was the producer of *Abe Lincoln in Illinois* and had co-produced the Pulitzer-Prize-winning play *Our Town,* and he worked in moving pictures as well as theater. He told me about a wonderful dentist in Hollywood who took care of the movie stars. He thought I ought to bring Jimmy out there for surgery.

I did take my son to California; while we were there, Sam came out for a visit. I think I would have gone back to him, for we were really good friends, and Jimmy wanted us to get back together. But three days after Sam returned to Kentucky, he had a fatal heart attack.

Sam Conner had been a wonderfully good and kind person. It was just that he didn't enjoy the way I lived and I didn't enjoy the way he lived. Neither way was wrong—they were just different.

Jimmy's health remained a problem. He couldn't walk—he was partially paralyzed from an injury to his neck. I had taken him to every type of doctor imaginable, but none was able to help him. Finally, one day, a New York friend of mine suggested I try a man he had heard about by the name of Edgar Cayce, who was, in fact, from my state of Kentucky.

"I'll try anything to help Jimmy get well," I said.

My friend arranged for me to speak with Mr. Cayce by phone. Edgar Cayce told me to take my son to Clearwater,

Florida, and check into a certain hotel. I was to walk Jimmy into the ocean as many times a day as I could.

My mother and father went with us. Papa fished, and Mama and Jimmy sunbathed between the hours of Jimmy's treatments, while I caught up with my reading. It was a wonderful time for the four of us. In three months' time, Jimmy had regained control of his arms and legs.

Mr. Cayce also had some warnings for my son. He said that Jimmy should never drink anything alcoholic because he believed his liver had been damaged in the wreck.

Soon after my return from Florida, I moved alone to a maisonette at 960 Fifth Avenue. It was very difficult to reach a settlement with McInnerney, and the proceedings of my divorce dragged on and on. McInnerney would not agree to my terms until he realized that one of the witnesses was a doctor who had treated me while we were living together— he'd had to stitch my lip as a result of McInnerney's brutality. The settlement then came in a hurry.

My marriage to McInnerney had lasted less than a year. He listed me as his second wife in the 1942-43 edition of *Who's Who in America,* but in the in 1946-47 edition I had been expunged and my place as second wife had been taken by Emma Adams.

It was because of me that he had gotten into *Who's Who* in the first place. When I was in Washington, a Mr. Cassini, whom I knew as the designer Oleg Cassini's brother, was a writer for a newspaper in the socially elite city of Warrenton, Virginia. Mr. Cassini had written an unflattering article about a prominent socialite, and he was practically ridden out of town on a rail. I stood up for him.

This Mr. Cassini was to write under the name of Cholly Knickerbocker when he got to New York. Cholly controlled the social scene in New York City. He never forgot that I defended him, so in turn he placed me on the social register.

Now at last I was free from this terrible man, and I could concentrate on putting together a staff for my new home. I sent to Kentucky for a cook, and, in answer to my call, there came the divine Mary Scott Crowe. Mary Scott was such an excellent cook that Somerset Maugham used to phone from Paris or Hawaii to see if I still had her. I always said, "Yes, and I guess you want to come to dinner just to see Mary Scott and taste the food she always prepares for you."

"Oh, thank you," Maugham would say softly. "I'll call you when I reach New York." He always did. He loved Mary Scott and so did I.

It was while I was living in my New York apartment that I heard over the radio that President Roosevelt had died while he was in Georgia and his body would be brought back home on a funeral train.

Most people probably did not know about Franklin Roosevelt's involvement with another woman until he died with her at his side. Of course, all of us who had been close to him knew that he had shared her love since they'd met when he was assistant secretary of the navy. Theirs was a deep, deep relationship.

On the day the train was to arrive in New York City, I stood at the window of my apartment, listening to the somber toll of a church bell. I just couldn't seem to make myself go to the railway station to view his body. But, then, I knew I must.

I stood waiting with the crowd. No one spoke a word. Only the tear-filled eyes of the people told of the sorrow each of us felt. Then we heard what to me was the most lonesome sound in the world. The train's whistle came from the distance, first as a soft moan, then closer and closer until its cry seemed to wrench our hearts in two. We all moved as one toward the track, desperately wanting to see Franklin Roosevelt, unable to believe that death could conquer someone who was bigger than life.

A single voice began to sing: "Going home, going home, I'm just going home." One by one we all joined in as the train eased to a stop.

The railway car carrying his body was made entirely of glass. The president lay on his bier, completely visible. The floor of the car was covered with roses and the American flag floated gently over him.

As I stood there, my thoughts flashed back to the afternoons when President Roosevelt gathered some of his closest associates around the pool. Harry Hopkins, Marvin McIntyre, Missy LeHand, and some of the Roosevelt family were usually there at this time, which had become the president's hour of relaxation. It was on one of these occasions that he announced that he had a special job for "Baby" to do in his administration and asked me to work as Hopkins's assistant.

"I will do anything you ask," I had answered then. But later, there was that one time when he asked too much; I, sorrowfully, had to tell him I could not, in good, conscience, support him for a third term. I never again saw him in person. And now, as I stared at him lying in the glass-enclosed railway car, I remembered all the wondrous things he had done for his country, guiding us through terrible times.

I soon settled back into the social whirl of New York City, enjoying the theater, opera, the symphony, fashion shows, and the wonderful restaurants. But my life was about to undergo another drastic change. Harry Goetz divorced his wife and asked me to marry him.

13

Hollywood Years

WHEN I MOVED TO CALIFORNIA, I kept my apartment in New York for the excitement and cultural events of the winter season. But I found summer in California, with its perfect climate, delightful. Southern California and Beverly Hills were beautiful, with their wonderfully clean beaches and large swimming pools.

The lifestyle in the tinsel world of movieland and movie magnates was certainly a far cry from what I was used to in Washington and New York. In 1943 culture had not yet descended. The one great restaurant was Romanoff's, and there one went to see and be seen and was never disappointed. The days were filled with luncheons at Romanoff's, cocktails around someone's pool, and dinner either at someone's home or back at Romanoff's. At first I loved it.

Since I now had plenty of money of my own, I put a down payment on a house high in the mountains on Chalon Road in Bel Air. The vivid view from my bedroom balcony showed both the ocean and the city of Los Angeles spread like a carpet of jewels at my feet. And the sunsets were magnificent!

But Harry insisted that he wanted to provide me with a home. Finally, we agreed that I would pay the house off and he would give me his note for that amount, which I put in our joint lock box.

The Goetz family into which I'd married were truly moguls in the movie industry. His brother Bill, whose wife was the daughter of Louis B. Mayer, was the head of Universal Studios. Ben headed MGM in London, and Jack and Charlie produced films in Canada.

Bill and Edie Mayer Goetz lived next door to Gloria Swanson's house, which Joe Kennedy had bought her. Though I had served with Joe Kennedy on Franklin Roosevelt's finance committee, we were not social friends. I found him crude and distasteful. But there is one amusing story concerning him that I always remember.

President Roosevelt had a wonderful sense of humor. One day he summoned Joe Kennedy to his office; he was going to surprise him with the announcement that he was about to be appointed ambassador to England. Knowing that the traditional formal dress of the English had tight-fitting trousers, the president first asked Mr. Kennedy to turn around and drop his pants. With a quizzical look on his face, Kennedy obeyed. Mr. Roosevelt then informed him that he simply wanted to see what his legs would look like in tight-fitting English trousers when he became ambassador.

My house was next door to Cecil B. DeMille's, but I hardly knew my neighbors. This caused a bit of a problem for me one Thanksgiving morning. I had invited several guests for Thanksgiving dinner, and I had ordered a fresh turkey, which I was going to cook myself, as I had given the servants the holiday off. But I had expected them to have the turkey prepared for me. Well, it *was* plucked, but that was all.

I did know that a doctor lived on the other side of me, and I thought surely he would know how to gut a turkey. So I carried the bird to this neighbor's house. The maid opened the door. She had no idea who I was and gave me no time to explain.

"Get out of here, you scalawag!" she cried. "I don't want to buy a turkey."

On I continued, house to house along Chalon Road, with equally ungratifying results, until I came to the house at the foot of the hill. I had no idea who lived there. When the door opened, to my surprise there stood Cary Grant.

My mouth hung open as I stared at that wonderfully handsome man. Finally, I decided I had nothing to lose, so I asked him if he could gut a turkey.

"Sure," he said. "Come on in."

After he had successfully done the job, I asked how I could repay him. He was alone that day, so he asked if he might come to my dinner. I never had another party there without asking him.

I had been so busy with my Washington and New York life that most people on the Hollywood scene were unfamiliar to me, at least at first. One night at a dinner party I was seated next to a man I didn't know, so I asked him his name.

"Walt Disney," he replied.

"What do you do?" I wanted to know.

"Oh, I don't do anything, ma'am," he said, smiling. "The banks do it all for me."

I got to see the other side of California one night when I had arrived home around 2:00 A.M. I'd been in bed about an hour when I awakened with a sick feeling of fright. I reached for my bedside lamp, only to feel it gently pulling away from me. My heart jumped into my throat—a burglar! Then I heard the swish, swish of my swimming pool, as though a giant hand were stirring it to create big waves. I heard the waves splashing over the balustrade that surrounded the pool. I grabbed the lamp and turned it on. As I did, I saw the huge mirror over the mantel sway toward me from across the room. At the same time I heard screams from the servants' rooms and saw lights flashing on the mountain across from my mountain. Then I knew! I was having my first experience with an earthquake.

Running onto my balcony, I saw, three stories below, by

the light of a setting moon, the waves in my swimming pool arch over the four-foot wall around it into my garden. The trees on the opposite mountain swayed first to the left, then to the right. It was a frighteningly strong quake, but my house had been well built and I suffered no real damage beyond broken mirrors and glasses in the bar off the pool. Some people in California claimed not to be so scared of earthquakes, but I never got over my fear of them.

I had been living in Bel Air about six months when I was invited to Sir Charles and Lady Mendl's charming house in Beverly Hills. I had not met them, but my friend Cobina Wright, the columnist, was a good friend of the Mendls' and she had asked them to invite me.

When I walked in that night, I was overjoyed to find that Lady Mendl was the friend I had met as Elsie de Wolf at Elizabeth Marbury's house in 1932, my first day in New York for the finance committee meeting. I remembered that we said we would meet again someday, and now here we were in Hollywood ten years later. Much had happened to both of us since.

The Mendls had lived in Paris for several years, but when the Germans occupied France they escaped to the United States and settled in Beverly Hills. Elsie and Sir Charles maintained the nearest thing to a salon in that part of California, and the important people who flowed through their drawing room came from all over the world. It was at their house that I met the Alfred Lunts, the great acting couple. Irene Dunne was a friend of theirs, as was Ethel Barrymore, whose son, Sammy Colt, I often found beside my pool when I returned home in the afternoons. He loved my butler's old-fashioneds.

One weekend, Harry and I received an invitation to the opening of the meet at Del Mar, the racetrack Bing Crosby, Pat O'Brien, and Bill Quigley had started. I think they invited everybody in Hollywood.

When we got there, I thought they'd have our rooms ready.

"I forgot all about the rooms," Bing sighed. "I'm having a hell of a time because I forgot so many details."

He instructed us to go on to the track and he'd see what he could do. After the races, Bing did come through. He said he had a little yacht that held just two people, and Harry and I could sleep there. Since we wanted to be at Del Mar for the next day's racing, we accepted his invitation. He told us where the yacht was and phoned ahead to confirm the arrangements for Harry, me, and Eddie, our chauffeur.

We found the dock, but the yacht was really more of a one-man boat. It did have an upstairs and a little downstairs. I had the downstairs, Harry took the upstairs, and Eddie had to sleep on the deck.

Bing and Bill were supposed to be sleeping on a big yacht somewhere on the water, but at about three in the morning came a great WHOOM, WHOOM, and waves, and a horn blowing. Harry fell out of his berth into the water and Eddie went right off the deck into the bay. Both of them began to yell and scream. As I was the only one who could swim, I had to leap in to try to rescue both of them.

Bing and the others on his yacht realized what they had done, and they came back and finally got us all back on board our boat. I don't know when I ever spent a more horrible night.

The 1940s and 1950s were the heyday of the gossip columnists in Hollywood. Hedda Hopper and Louella Parsons were the better-known ones, but a latecomer to the group was my friend Cobina Wright. Hedda and Louella tended to write with barbed-wire pens, while Cobina wrote gaily and happily. She was also by far the most beautiful of the three.

It was at Mary Pickford's house, Pickfair, named for her and her first husband, Douglas Fairbanks, that the long-smoldering feud between Cobina and Hedda Hopper broke out into the open. Mary and her second husband, Buddy Rogers, were giving a cocktail party one Thursday evening. Harry and I were asked, along with my son Jimmy and his wife, Frances, who were visiting me. We arrived to find ourselves in the midst of a top-drawer group made up of the leading men and women of the cinema world, famous hostesses and hosts, mighty businessmen, high society, the publishing world, and beautiful women. Even by Hollywood standards, it was a gala affair.

Also, there were the three leading columnists. Cobina, Hedda, and Louella wrote from different angles, but among them they managed to tell who was who and what was what and give those tantalizing bits of gossip that titillated the fans of Hollywood. They usually covered all the important parties and places separately, but they met that night in the star-studded drawing rooms and gardens of Pickfair. Louella was in one drawing room seated on a couch surrounded by fans, and Hedda was in an adjoining room with her group when Cobina appeared.

She arrived rather late, just when she calculated that the party would be in full swing. She swept in, head high, brown eyes wide, and smiling—and saw Hedda.

Both Cobina and Hedda had bought what they'd been told was an "original" gown. In Hollywood, two "originals" just *couldn't* happen! But they did, and the two rivals had bought the same low-cut, silver satin "original."

Without changing her expression, Cobina accepted a brimming glass of champagne, walked over to Hedda, and, bending down as if to kiss her, poured the champagne down the décolletage of Hedda's gown.

Such commotion! Hedda jumped up, overturning some of her fans in her haste, looked down and saw her ruined dress, and spat out at the wickedly grinning Cobina, "You clumsy fool—I'll make hash of you yet!"

In the next day's papers, neither Hedda nor Louella mentioned the incident, but Cobina wrote one of her most inspired descriptions of the evening, ending with the statement, "Never have I enjoyed myself more."

One of my dearest friends in Hollywood was Maureen O'Sullivan, the Jane of the early Tarzan movies, wife of writer John Farrow and mother of actress Mia Farrow. Maureen became an almost daily visitor to my house when one of my old friends from Kentucky came for a stay.

I had heard that Dan Talbott was in Arizona for health reasons, so I sent for him to come to Bel Air and I gave him a room by the pool. Maureen loved to visit with him; they would talk for hours.

Dan's health seemed to be improving over the weeks so he decided to go back to Kentucky. His marriage had broken up, and I was concerned that he had nowhere to live when he got home. I phoned my mother, and she readily agreed that he could live with her. But Dan never got there. He made an overnight stop in Louisville and was found the next morning in his room, dying of a heart attack.

As the glitter of tinsel-town life gradually paled, I looked around for something more interesting than the lazy party life to occupy me. Then Conrad Hilton presented me with a rare opportunity. He asked me to serve as a member of the executive board of the Los Angeles United Nations Day Committee. This observance of United Nations Day was the first of what we hoped would become a worldwide holiday, embracing all races, faiths, and nations and dedicated to universal peace.

I served with Ronald Colman on a committee that brought the Sadlers Wells Ballet of London to southern California. Jimmy Stewart and I were on a cancer awareness committee. I got on various boards and committees nationwide.

I often found myself mentioned in the columns. Cobina named me, in her column in *Screenland* magazine, as one of eight outstanding Hollywood hostesses. The others were Mary

Pickford, Greer Garson, Joan Crawford, Joan Bennett, Gene Tierney, Sonja Henie, and Mrs. Peter Rathvon. Walter Thornton chose me to be on his list of ten American Beauties, all of us over the age of thirty.

But the political scene was about to enter my life again. In 1950, I received a letter from former president Herbert Hoover, asking for my support for a senatorial candidate in the state of California. I liked and trusted Mr. Hoover so I took his word that Richard Nixon would make a good senator.

I began to talk with some of the people in the movie industry, including Harry Brand of Twentieth Century Fox and writer Adela Rogers St. John. I said I could organize the campaign—I'd been doing that all my life—and St. John and Brand said they'd get behind it.

I spent a day calling my friends in Hollywood to ask for their support, and that evening after dinner I told my husband that I was going to organize the "Independent Voters for Nixon." Harry said he thought it was a good idea.

The next day I called Hernando Courtright, manager of the Beverly Hills Hotel, and asked if we could rent a room for our headquarters. He let us have three rooms at no charge, and he picked up the tab for the telephone.

My friends and I built up a wonderful political organization in Beverly Hills and Los Angeles. Some of the members were well-known personalities; they included the Farrows, Hedda and Cobina, Mr. and Mrs. Dick Powell, Mr. and Mrs. Joseph Cotton, Mr. and Mrs. George Murphy, Mr. and Mrs. Lauritz Melchior, Mr. and Mrs. Adolph Menjou, Rosalind Russell, Hoagy Carmichael, Ann Southern, Ward Bond, and Jeanette MacDonald. Even my cook Helen organized the black community. Everything broke right. The newspapers began to give us coverage, and Mr. Nixon won his senatorial election.

Then, in the latter part of 1951, things began to fall apart in my personal life. Harry Goetz and I were to meet with a group of friends in Colorado Springs. I was driving because Harry didn't know how to drive. I was tense, thinking about whether to accept an invitation to get even more deeply involved in politics.

I'd asked Harry to read the road map and give me directions. All of a sudden, we came to a place where there was a choice of ways to Colorado Springs. One route was through the mountains and the other was on more level ground. I hated mountain driving; when I realized that Harry had directed me onto the more mountainous route, I lost my temper.

"You can't even read a road map," I snapped. "Can't you do anything right?"

Of course, he became very angry, and we argued. He told me he resented my always being away from home. He hated the idea that I was thinking about accepting an offer to campaign in the presidential election. Finally, he said he didn't care what I did anymore.

I said I didn't care either. But that's when my decision was made. I would definitely campaign for General Dwight D. Eisenhower in his run for the presidency.

When we arrived in Colorado Springs, Harry began to belittle me in front of our friends. I asked him what was wrong with him, and he gave me a certain look. I knew that look. It meant he had done something, and I somehow knew it had to do with the money he owed me for our house.

From Colorado, Harry flew to New York and I drove alone back to Beverly Hills. I went straight to our bank, where I knew one woman employee very well. I said I wanted to look in my lock box. She told me that Harry had come to the bank a few days before with his former wife and that they had looked through our box. The note he had given me for his payment on the house was not there. I had been warned to make a copy, but I hadn't, and now my money was gone.

Looking back on my marriage with Harry Goetz, I believe he very much wanted prestige, which always seemed to elude him. He had helped to raise his younger brother, William, and now it was Bill and not he who was head of a major movie studio.

Harry had been so nice when I first met him, and I fell in love with him. But as time progressed, I believe a sickness started working on him. Something that happened with Harry's son confirmed my belief. Walter was a wonderful young man. I loved him and he was almost as dear as my own son. Walter had suffered terribly from a bout of polio as a young person, and it was very difficult for him to walk. Once he and Harry got into an argument, and Harry knocked him down. If Harry could do that to his disabled son, he could surely turn on me. I knew I had to get out of the marriage.

My return to national politics promised the respite I desperately needed. Soon I was heading back to Washington, D.C., to begin my part in the Eisenhower campaign. I stopped on the way to see Oral Roberts and told him that Richard Nixon, who was now running with General Eisenhower for the position of vice-president, had sent me. I told him that I had worked in Washington and spoke of the things I was going to do in the campaign.

He told me of his plans to build a church like no one had ever seen before and showed me an exquisite stained-glass window he had for it of Christ weeping in the garden. I asked him if he had raised any money toward the building, and he said he had. So I asked if he could financially help the Eisenhower-Nixon campaign. He said he certainly could and handed me a hundred-dollar bill.

I drove on to Washington, where I met with Senator Owen Brewster of Maine and several others. I told them I was there to help and that I had a little money of my own. They said they would donate a thousand dollars toward my expenses if I would go to the southern states to campaign.

I was sent to a ranch at Yemasee, South Carolina, between Beaufort and Charleston. The owner was an heiress to the

Kresge fortune. People soon heard about me; I was written up in several newspapers. They began to call, asking me for speaking engagements.

The South was still notoriously Democratic. It was unusual for southerners to vote Republican so we kept the name of "Independent Voters for Eisenhower." I got into a little trouble when I told people that Bernard Baruch, once a financial adviser to Roosevelt, was for Eisenhower. He didn't want to admit it, but he was. He gave me a good tongue-lashing. Harry Byrd got mad, too. He called me up and said not to tell anyone that he was for Eisenhower.

Working for General Eisenhower occupied my time completely. For months, I campaigned for him in the South, gradually pulling votes away from the Democratic candidate.

I had first been introduced to General Eisenhower at the Hollywood Bowl. He commented that he thought I had the gift of gab. But for the most part, I was not close with the Eisenhowers. It was through my association with Richard Nixon that I had gotten interested in the presidential campaign.

I spotted right away that Nixon was ambitious, and I did not like him personally. I did, however, admire Eisenhower, and I always felt that Nixon was jealous of him. The Nixons were not the kind of people you would have for dinner—they were not a fun couple to be with. I did find Pat Nixon to be a lovely person but very retiring.

Mamie Eisenhower was different. She was fun. Her favorite pastimes were drinking and playing bridge. She often played bridge with the sister of Steve Early, who was a friend of mine, and he kept me filled in on what was happening with the Eisenhowers.

After the success of the campaign, I asked for a special appointment. There was one place I'd always wanted to go but had never had the opportunity. I very much wanted to see Europe.

14

Assignment in Europe

IN 1954 I LEFT CALIFORNIA to return to Washington, which has always felt more like home to me than anywhere else, even Kentucky. I went to see Vice-President Richard Nixon, who was very kind and gave me valuable advice as to how to go about getting a government position in Europe. I didn't want to be an ambassador but a roving promoter of U.S. interests.

Mr. Nixon made an appointment for me to see President Eisenhower, who listened and questioned me. One of the many things President Eisenhower was expert at was the art of listening. After a long discussion, he suggested that I might be interested in the U.S. expansion into the field of industrial trade fairs, which was being overseen by the Department of Commerce. He also suggested I call on Secretary of State John Foster Dulles. He not only suggested it, he rang for his secretary and set up the appointment personally.

Mr. Dulles was a most delightful man. In the course of conversation, we discovered that we had a mutual friend, Hugh Gibson, the ambassador to Switzerland.

My acquaintance with Hugh Gibson had begun in 1952. After the election, I had gone to New York to work with him on a French film about the life of Christ that was to be a joint effort between French producers and Hugh Gibson and me as the American co-producers. We set up a secretarial staff in

New York; in the few months I stayed there to work on the project—which unfortunately did not come to fruition—I came to respect and admire him greatly.

Secretary Dulles told me that Hugh was not well; he suggested that if I went to Europe, I should go to Geneva at once because he feared Hugh might not live long. But I did not get to see him again. To my great regret, Hugh Gibson died the night I arrived in Paris.

Dulles then suggested that his brother Allen, who was with the Commerce Department, might be able to give me an assignment. When I saw him, Allen Dulles explained that his department was planning to arrange to present American goods at various ports in Europe. He wondered if I would be interested in looking around Italy and France to select those ports for them.

Another dream was coming true. I would soon be in Europe. But the more I thought about it, the more I dreaded going alone. There were advantages to being married. And there was an obvious candidate.

I'd first met Robert Savage when Cobina Wright brought him to a party at my house in California. He had a wonderful war record as one of General Claire Chennault's Flying Tigers, and that impressed me greatly. He was also a singer and had made several records.

Bob wanted to go to Europe, too. At that time he was interested in developing the idea of frozen juice concentrate, and he wanted to survey plants in Italy and perhaps set up a business in Europe. He had no money for the trip, and I preferred not to go alone so marriage appeared to be the solution. Off we went to Mexico for the ceremony.

Before leaving for Europe, we stopped in Washington, D.C. From our hotel, I took a walk to one of my favorite places, the Tidal Basin, where the beautiful cherry trees bloom in the spring. But this was December, and the trees stood bare against a gray sky.

As I walked along, a familiar figure approached. I prepared to speak to him, but he only stared at me with his black, intense eyes. I was so taken aback I was unable to speak. Shaken, I returned to the hotel, where I related the unsettling experience to Bob. It was with that chance meeting at the tidal basin that I received an insight into the soul of Richard Nixon. From that day on I knew the man was capable of doing something awful.

Bob and I found that if we hurried our preparations for leaving, we could be in Paris for Christmas. I rushed to store trunks and pack personal belongings. I still am of the opinion that taking only two medium-sized suitcases for a trip that might be from three months up to two years, winter and summer, rain or shine, puts me in the all-time genius class of packing and planning.

Unfortunately, we didn't realize that tourist class allows only thirty pounds of baggage per person. It had been Bob's idea to fly tourist to save a little money, but when I'd phoned to inquire how much weight we were permitted, I forgot to mention that we were going tourist. Assuming we were going first class, the agent quoted sixty pounds per person.

When we weighed in at Idlewild, Bob came as near to fainting as a healthy, six-foot-four man could when he found out we'd have to pay a hundred dollars extra for excess baggage. It turned out we could have gone first class in comfort and come out about even in cost.

After Bob got over his shock, he settled down in the plane and began to relax, something I was unable to do. I ached from head to toe because Bob had made me carry on a bag he positively refused to weigh in. This particular bag was actually the heaviest of our luggage because it contained his hair oil (twenty-four bottles), his books of publicity, his sheet music, and his records, but that didn't seem to concern him as he watched me stagger from the terminal to the plane. It was his notion that I could get away with carrying it on—a woman wouldn't be likely to be carrying something very heavy—whereas he might be stopped; and I was silly enough to undertake to do it.

There he stood on the steps of the plane, free of bundles and baggage, smiling and looking handsome and superior, giving every appearance of having no connection with the lumbering human tank struggling unsteadily up the plane steps. Later, he explained that he would have been embarrassed if I had been stopped and weighed. *He* would have been embarrassed!

Soon he was asleep, but whenever he awakened as we crossed the Atlantic, he would look at me and ask, "Are you sure you know how to speak French?"

"Of course," I assured him. "Haven't I been studying and listening to all those French records for almost six months? Don't worry. They'll think I was born in France."

He seemed doubtful, but he finally entered into the spirit of our trip, ordered me a martini, then pushed back his seat and dozed until our stop in Ireland. I was too tired and excited to sleep. I watched the night fade and experienced the uplift I have always felt at witnessing a sunrise.

As we landed at Shannon, our steward announced a thirty-minute stop. Out we climbed and headed toward the dining room in the terminal. Unfortunately, the thirty minutes stretched into four hours, delaying our arrival in Paris until late in the afternoon of Christmas Eve. By then, having had no sleep in thirty-six hours, I was so exhausted I could hardly keep my eyes open.

Another reason we'd decided to fly tourist was that by saving money we could afford to stay at the Georges V Hotel—I had friends who said they always stayed there so that's where we wanted to go, too. Having to pay for the excess baggage had scuttled that plan, but we'd told everyone we would be at the Georges V, so we went to the Georges V.

After we came through customs, Bob said, "Let's don't

worry about money now. We'll have a hell of a Christmas. Just tell the taxi driver where we want to go."

I opened my mouth, but not one word of French came out. I was in the throes of stage fright for the first time in my life. Bob looked at me and repeated, "Go on, honey, tell the man where we want to go." I began to stutter and point. Maybe I was punchy from fatigue, but I never said one word of French. To make matters worse, I couldn't understand a single word the taxi driver said.

"Well," Bob began, "I wondered all along if you could. . . ."

"Shut up," I stormed at him, frustrated at the memory of all those hours listening to the records. "I don't need you to tell me you 'knew all along!'"

By that time, we were both good and mad. I withdrew into a corner of the cab and left Bob to tell the driver where he wanted to go. Of course, he had been relying on me for the French, but he finally got it across to the man, though not until he was hoarse from shouting. Why do people always shout when trying to communicate in a foreign language?

It was four in the afternoon by the time we finally settled down in the bustling hotel. "Let's take a little nap so we can be fresh for Noel," said Bob, stretching himself out on one of those famously soft beds.

"Wonderful," I agreed, and I was asleep before my head touched the pillow.

When I awakened it was dark. I felt disoriented, and I had a terrible urge for breakfast. It was a strange experience to want breakfast at night. I looked at the clock and made out that it was five o'clock. Only one hour of sleep! I sank back into a stupor. Finally, I awoke again. It was still dark, only now the clock said four o'clock. How crazy can one get, I wondered, thoroughly confused.

"Bob," I called, "are you awake?"

"I am now," he said, slowly pushing back the covers. He at last managed to get his feet on the floor, and after holding his head in his hands for a few minutes, he staggered to the window and looked out. "It's dark outside," he said. "What time is it?"

"Four o'clock," I answered.

"In the morning?"

"Oh, Bob, I'm so confused," I cried. "Please ask the operator what time it is."

"You ask," he replied. "You're the one that speaks French so well that they'll think you were born here, remember?"

Reluctantly, I picked up the phone. Finally, some of the language came to me. "Quelle heure est-il?" I asked.

An English voice answered sleepily, "It's 4:00 A.M., Madame."

I hesitated as cold realization began to creep over me, then I weakly asked, "What day is it?"

With that, the voice of the operator came awake. In crisp tones she informed me politely and firmly that it was 4:00 A.M., the twenty-sixth of December.

We had slept through Christmas Eve and Christmas Day! Bob and I just looked at each other. So much for our Christmas in Paris.

But I did have some of social activity between then and New Year's. Elsie de Wolfe Mendl had died in 1950, and her husband, Sir Charles Mendl, had settled back in Paris. He had a dinner for me. And Earl Blackwell, who ran Celebrity Service, gave a cocktail party in my honor on New Year's Eve.

For some reason, Bob was furious about my going to this party. I knew Bob Savage had a mean streak when I married him—he wasn't afraid of anything. But I was mean, too. I thought I could hold my own with him. I was mistaken.

Just after the new year, it was time for me to go to Rome, but Bob was still sullen about the party and he refused to go. So I left him in Paris and started to Italy by train. I got off to a flying start by missing the Rome express out of Paris so I had to catch a later train with a stopover and change in Milan.

Having satisfactorily made my connection in Milan, I was at last on an express to Rome.

The train got under way and was soon flashing by the fields of northern Italy. The windows were steamy on the inside and rivulets of rain were running down the outside, but I found the scene enchanting. I was prepared to find everything about Italy enchanting—it reminded me so much of my beloved California. I'm going to love Italy and Rome, I said to myself. It was certainly a different feeling than I had had in France. I was a little frightened at being alone; but some adventurous ancestors had given me a stout heart, and I was actually looking forward to my tour of Italy alone, on my own.

I suddenly felt very hungry—not surprising since it was two in the afternoon and I hadn't eaten since lunch the day before in Paris. As I got up to leave my compartment, in popped a very handsome young man who introduced himself as the official in charge (conductor to us in the United States). Whatever he was saying was in Italian with about every third word in English. As he went on explaining with expressive waving of the hands and lifts of the eyebrows, smiles, and frowns, I finally got the point. He was informing me that he had to have some more money, because I was now traveling on an express and it was an extra-fare train.

Having not one word of Italian at my command (I hadn't been studying or listening to Italian records for the last six months), I opened my bag, dug out a handful of bills, and told him by gestures, a timid raising of my eyebrows, and a mild form of hand waving, to take what he wanted. He picked very carefully among the bills and selected what he needed, smiling sweetly all the time.

After settling with him, I began to point to my mouth while rubbing my stomach, hoping to convey to this likable young official that I was hungry. He readily understood and pointed toward the front of the train. With much bowing and many smiles, we parted, and I proceeded forward, hoping that I could find something on the Italian menu that I could recognize and pronounce. Having had no breakfast, what I really wanted was orange juice, two four-minute eggs, and coffee. In anticipation, I tripped lightheartedly through the cars and across the frightening intersections between them.

Arriving at the diner, I found it full of happy Italians, downing mountains of spaghetti, bottles of red wine, mounds of cheese, and baskets of fruit, topping it all off with coffee, sweets, and brandy. Everyone seemed in the holiday spirit of the new year. I was welcomed by a smiling captain and seated in the one and only remaining seat at a table already occupied by three men. Picking up the menu, I knew I was lost. Not an egg or a glass of orange juice could I spot. It was luncheon—breakfast was over.

By grunts and gestures I managed to place my order, and when the waiter left, puzzled but smiling, I settled back to await the results. Truthfully, I had no idea what I had ordered and was rather excited to see what I would be served.

After quite a delay, the food began to arrive. First a bottle of red wine, not a small bottle one would suppose a single person would order, but a liter. "No, no, not that," I protested, and the waiter, full of smiling apologies, took it away and brought me the same-sized bottle of white wine. In despair, I gave up on the size and with more grunts and gestures made it known that I wanted red and not white. Still smiling politely and happily, the waiter returned with the original big bottle of red wine, which I accepted. I felt my face take on a tinge of pink because of the surreptitious glances of the three men at my table who had already worked through their desserts and were now busy with their toothpicks.

The wine was only the start. Next came spaghetti and meat sauce with Parmesan cheese, followed by a heavy soup; then fish with potatoes, followed in rapid succession by veal in a cream sauce with mushrooms and peppers. By this time,

I was beginning to get quite warm, not only from the wine but from the curious glances of practically everyone in the car. Things worsened. Next came salad and cheese, fruit, figs, and nuts. Once, when I looked up, I discovered that the whole dining car had stopped eating and all were following, with amazement, every course served to me. Conversation had come to a halt.

The waiter, still bent on pleasing, sailed in with the most revolting dessert I ever saw—not that the tart topped with whipped cream and cherries wasn't a pastry chef's delight, but I was very, very full. Last came the rich espresso coffee. The waiter, perspiring but still smiling, kept refilling my glass with wine. When I chanced to look at the bottle I discovered, to my amazement, that it was almost empty. Could I possibly have drunk all that, I wondered. My eyes were becoming glazed over and I was fast approaching a drunken dizziness.

Finally, the meal was over. Everyone in the car heaved a sigh of relief. I could imagine what they were saying to themselves—"the American, what an appetite she has!"

Then came the bill—7,500 lira (more than $12 in American money). I'm sure it was the largest bill ever presented a lone diner on an Italian train, or any other train for that matter, in 1955. Even in my stupefied condition, I knew it was outrageous. I began feebly to protest. At that moment, up stepped two officials, resplendent in uniforms with shiny buttons. I gathered from their gestures that not only was I to pay this bill but also they were to collect the extra fare for the express.

This was too much! I began to talk louder and faster, explaining that I had already paid the extra fare and protesting that I had not ordered the luncheon I had been served—and, to my disgrace, eaten. One of my table companions seemed to understand and from his excited gestures I gathered he was defending me. The waiter and the two officials were definitely against me. One by one, the whole car got into the argument.

As well as I could follow, it was about fifty-fifty, some for me, some for the waiter and officials.

The debate grew louder and louder, until I cried, "Hush, hush! I'll pay everything if only you will stop this confounded noise!" With that, a dead silence fell on the car. I did not know if it was just the sound of my voice or whether they understood what I said, but you could have heard a pin drop. Even my defender seemed aghast.

After I paid the luncheon bill, the two officials each took an arm and began to escort me from the car. Our progress was followed by bright, angry looks from the waiter and his gang and solemn looks and mutterings from my champion. Down the five cars back to my compartment I was marched.

Arriving at the compartment, we went in and I sat down. So did the two officials. After a few minutes, I realized we were waiting for someone. Goodness me, I thought, I'm going to be arrested!

Gone was my affection for these happy Italians. Worry began to add itself to my other discomforts. I began to feel tremors of fright running up and down my spine, so I tried to console myself by saying this can't happen to me. I've done nothing wrong. But there I was, and it didn't look good.

Some twenty minutes later, I heard a hum of voices. Down the car came a string of people from the dining car, headed by my champion. In they marched and with them was the handsome young conductor to whom I'd paid the extra fare. At last the officials yielded and seemed convinced that I had already paid.

Then began the long and excited argument that the Italians love to indulge themselves in and are famous for. They stepped outside my compartment and went into a huddle. After some minutes they knocked on my door. Back came the two officials with the conductor, and with many smiles and much bowing they refunded *all* of the money—extra fare, the luncheon, the works! Even the tips!

When they did this, a triumphant shout arose from my champion and, pushing his way into my compartment, he seized my hand and kissed it, all the while murmuring, "So sorry, Madame Ambassador, so sorry."

Then it dawned on me. The way I'm dressed, they way I'm wearing my hair, I'm an American—they think I'm Claire Booth Luce, the U.S. ambassador to Italy. "Oh, no," I protested, "You've made a mistake. No, no." But to no avail. My friend rolled his big brown eyes at me and began his apologies again.

What could I do? Flashing my most engaging smile, I asked my defenders in, thanked them in the name of the United States, and invited them all to come see me at the embassy in Rome. I wonder if they ever showed up.

When I arrived in Rome I checked into the Excelsior Hotel, where I discovered that, in my haste to leave Paris, I had accidentally picked up some of Bob's luggage. I called him and said that I would send it back. He said no, he would come get it. When he appeared, I told him I thought it would be best if we dissolved our marriage. He was fifteen years younger than me, and our interests were not the same. He went on his way and I never heard from him again.

Later I moved to the Grand Hotel, which remained my principal headquarters until 1958. In the four years I was in Europe, I returned to the United States for some time each year to visit my family in Kentucky, where I began, in 1956, to get involved with promoting tourism and to advise the Commerce Department in Washington on sites for the industrial trade fairs. I recommended a total of twenty-two cities to be considered, and from that list eleven were chosen.

For years I had been feeling a pull toward a conversion to Catholicism, and Rome was certainly the right place to foster such an inclination. Close to the Grand Hotel was a church I loved to attend.

One busy day I returned to my room terribly tired, undressed, threw myself on the bed, immediately fell asleep, and had the most extraordinarily vivid dream.

I was walking down a long, narrow dirt road. On my right, a shallow, lazy river flowed gently with small waves lapping both sides. As I moved slowly and quietly down the road, I saw a small mountain on my left, ledges of rock, layer upon layer, rising up and up and out of sight. Then a light appeared on my left side and moved along with me. There was complete silence. Even the waves were silent. I gazed down the road. Suddenly, I saw golden gates opening and heard a voice saying, "This is the Jordan River." Then I woke up.

The next morning, going down for breakfast, I stopped at the desk and asked if anyone knew where the Jordan River was and how to get there. The man who set up tours smiled, said, "Just a minute," and picked up the phone. After a brief consultation, he told me that it could be reached by air in just a few hours and that a plane was leaving shortly for Tel Aviv. There I could get a car and driver who could take me to the Jordan.

I caught the plane and, upon landing in Tel Aviv, found a driver who said he knew where the mouth of the Jordan was and he could take me there. We drove over narrow, dusty roads and finally I saw a shallow stream. The driver stopped and stepped out, opened my door, bowed low, and said dramatically, "This is the mouth of the Jordan River."

I told the driver I was going to walk along it. I couldn't believe it! There was the narrow dirt road, the small mountain of ledges of rock reaching up out of sight, the river moving slowly. The stillness. Not a sound. I walked on down the road, and suddenly a light appeared on my left and moved with me. I reached out my hand. There was nothing there, only the light. Then I saw a plank by side of the road that read, "This is the Jordan River."

I returned to the car; the driver looked at me and asked, "Are you all right?"

"Yes," I replied, but I told him about the light and the plank.

He stood looking down the road and said, "I've never seen that plank, but I've brought many visitors here; in one group there was a young boy of six or seven who said he saw a hand and a plank there." We looked at each other. "I don't understand it," he added. Neither did I. As we returned to Tel Aviv, we were very quiet.

I was fortunate in finding a plane leaving for Rome. When I returned to the Grand Hotel after this extraordinary experience, I needed a long rest and had a great deal of thinking to do.

The next day I called Father James Cunningham at Santa Susanna, the American Catholic church in Rome. I had gotten an introduction to him from the abbot at the Trappist monastery of Gethsemani near Bardstown. When I called on Father Cunningham, I found we had many mutual acquaintances, and he was very helpful to me. I felt I should tell him the story of the Jordan River. I told him the whole story, the dream and the corresponding reality. He listened without saying a word. I finished and waited. It was not long before he spoke in a low voice.

"Catherine," he said, which surprised me, as he had always called me Mrs. Conner, "I would like to take you to the Holy Father and have you tell him your story. Will you go?" I became frightened, but I trusted Father Cunningham and agreed to go.

He made the arrangements for me to have a private audience with Pope Pius XII, and he took me to the Vatican. As we approached the pope's office, the door opened and there he stood, in a white robe and a gold and crimson cape. Around his neck was a gold chain from which hung a magnificent jeweled cross. Seen so close, he was tall, with black eyes and a receding forehead. He smiled and bowed his head. No one had instructed me how to greet such an important person, so

I bowed very low. He came forward and placed his hand on my arm and raised me up.

Father Cunningham left, and Pope Pius seated me in front of his desk. He looked at me for a full two minutes, maybe more, then he began to question me, first about Abbot Fox and President Eisenhower; then, as he saw that I had gotten more relaxed, he asked about my dream.

I told him. When I finished, he asked me more questions. I told him everything, my childhood, my four husbands, my mistakes, my sorrows, my sins big and small. I found myself on my knees, crying and pleading. Then, to my astonishment, I said, "I want to become a Catholic."

He helped me to my feet and said, "Rest, my child, Father Cunningham and I will help you."

I faltered. "What must I do? Go to confession?"

His smile was gentle. "You have been to confession, my dear. You are forgiven, and to celebrate I am giving you my Bible. Study it, and when you read it, remember Rome and the church."

In 1958, I received a phone call from Dr. Morris Flexner in Louisville. My son Jimmy was dying. The doctor advised me to come to Kentucky at once. I left Rome that very night, never to return.

15

Return to Kentucky

To MY SURPRISE, Jimmy met me at the airport. He did not look ill, much less near death. He had endured so much after his accident—two months in a coma, facial reconstruction, and the treatment suggested by Edgar Cayce—that it was a miracle he had recovered enough to lead a normal life. I was sure he could be healthy again. I asked for a second opinion. It was the same. My son was dying of cirrhosis of the liver.

I didn't want to distress Jimmy with my fears for him so I decided not to come home to Bardstown. Instead, I moved to Lexington, where I was still close enough to keep an eye on him.

To occupy my mind with something other than worrying about Jimmy, I became more active in promoting tourism in Kentucky. My friend Happy Chandler had been elected to another term as governor. In 1958 he appointed me to the newly formed Tourism Bureau.

One day I was discussing with Lee McClain, former attorney general of Kentucky, the fact that Governor Chandler had asked me to suggest some ways to increase tourism in the state. I brought up the idea of outdoor dramas. When I was in Europe, I had seen a performance of an outdoor dramatization of *The Book of Job* in Brussels, Belgium, and thought it was excellent. I later tracked down the writer and producer, Orlin Corey, and talked to him by phone at some length. He had consented to go with me to Pineville, Kentucky, when he returned to the United States and discuss with the citizens of Pineville the possibility of doing the play there.

I asked Lee what he thought of the idea of an outdoor drama for Bardstown honoring Stephen Foster. He thought it was a terrific idea so I set out under the direction of Laban Jackson, the commissioner of conservation under Governor Chandler, to explore the possibilities of getting the citizens of Bardstown to support the idea. Many at first thought it was unworkable, but with the help of Mayor Frank Wilson and his wife, Elizabeth, plans were finally formed to promote it.

In Berea, Kentucky, I found Ted Cronk, who represented Paul Green, author of outdoor dramas for Virginia and elsewhere. Cronk thought Green would be interested in writing the play.

Money for building the amphitheater, promotion, and other expenses had to be raised quickly. I suggested to Elizabeth Wilson that she organize "one hundred friends of Stephen Foster." Most of the "friends" I suggested contacting had been guests for the first–day sale of the Stephen Foster commemorative stamp back in 1940 and seemed happy to be considered friends. Elizabeth and her committee successfully extracted $100 from each of them for promotion seed money, promising to return it if the drama wasn't produced.

Now it was up Labe Jackson and me to pry $50,000 toward building the amphitheater from Governor Chandler, who was the watchdog of public monies. Our task was to turn his "maybe" into a definite "yes." Finally he consented.

I selected the site, a perfect natural amphitheater on the grounds of My Old Kentucky Home. I could remember Jimmy and his friends camping out there when he was a boy and thought it would be a beautiful spot for such a gay, glamorous play as Paul Green promised. Governor Chandler named the theater the J. Dan Talbott Amphitheater in honor of our longtime friend.

Finally the night of the first performance came, and we were barely ready. Right before curtain time, Paul was on his knees in front of the stage, pushing sods of grass into place.

Both *The Stephen Foster Story* and *The Book of Job* opened in 1959, and both met great success. *The Book of Job* ran for the next twenty–five years, drawing viewers from around the world. *The Stephen Foster Story* is still running, bringing an abundance of visitors and revenue to Bardstown every summer.

I also helped the monastery near Bardstown at Gethsemani, which was having financial problems and needed a way to raise money. To me, the answer was obvious. In their kitchen they baked the most wonderful fruitcakes for Christmas. Why not sell them? I called my friend Conrad Hilton. His hotels were located all over the world and served good food. Why not serve this unique and delicious fruitcake? He agreed, and his order led to the making of a million dollars for Gethsemani. The fruitcake business is still the main source of revenue for the monastery, which continues to ship them all over the world.

In 1960, Jimmy's worsening condition convinced me to return to Bardstown to be close to him. I moved in with my mother in the cottage off the town square where I had lived when I first married.

Jimmy lingered on until 1963. March 18 was a windy night; rough rain beat on the windows of the hospital, lightning flashed, and thunder rattled the doors and windows. Jimmy was semiconscious. He had always been fond of classical music so I had brought his phonograph and records to the hospital with him. Beethoven's Fifth Symphony was playing when Jimmy spoke to me. "Mother, please turn the music off," he said. "I can't concentrate." I walked over and cut it off. When I turned back, he was gone. He was forty–two years old.

Jimmy gave me my only truly happy days. He was a beautiful baby, a beautiful little boy, a charming young man, a handsome man who died in his prime. As a child, he went first to public schools, then, at eleven, to a military school in Columbia, Tennessee. But living in Washington, D.C., I became so lonesome for him that he transferred to St. James School in Hagerstown, Maryland, so I could be near him. He stayed there two years but returned to Columbia to graduate. Then he entered college at the University of Virginia until the war, and his enlistment cut that short—and then the accident from which he never fully recovered.

He left me two grandsons, though: Sam, my trusted adviser and business manager, and Jimmy Dan, the fifth James in the family, and they have given me four great–grandchildren, Caroline, Frances Clay, James Daniel, and Katelyn.

Jimmy's tombstone reads:

Young, handsome, good!
A loving father
A devoted son
A loyal friend
James Daniel Conner.

After my son's death, I continued to live with my mother until she left me in 1970. Papa had died in 1944. Only one dear friend was left now; and, no matter where in the world he was, he phoned me every Sunday afternoon. Then one day in 1976 I opened the *New York Times,* and there was his name in the headlines—Jim Farley was dead.

The little cottage off the square in Bardstown grew silent, and in that silence I began to reflect, sifting through the faded clippings and pictures and letters I had saved over the years. Often my memories come in response to the whistle of a far–off train in the night. Over the years I had put down on paper some of my recollections, writing of things as though they had happened yesterday—but they happened many years ago.

For fifty years I did public service, devoting myself to civic affairs. Along with success and happiness had come heart-aches and failure. I had learned to accept all the vicissitudes of fortune—bereavement, poverty, humiliation, and pain.

In 1980 I sold the cottage and moved to an apartment on the campus at Nazareth, where I had gone to high school two–thirds of a century earlier, and where I had finally finished college in the late 1960s. I became a follower of Epictetus, with a slight difference. I now wanted to become a true re-cluse, devoting myself to contemplation, meditation, and prayer. I did this for ten years. Then I began to suffer from a series of pin strokes. When I woke up after the last one, I found myself in the Colonial House Nursing Home in Bardstown.

I have always been able to adapt to most any situation. I have now resigned myself to the fact that I live in a nursing home, though I never believed I would be at this point in my life. When we are young and strong we don't think of grow-ing old and fragile.

Much of my time is spent reading—thank God, I still have good eyesight. Once in a while, out–of–town acquaintances come to visit. I see my grandsons and their families. One great-grandchild is my namesake. I still receive requests to speak, and I stay in contact with the people connected with My Old Kentucky Home. I was pleased to attend and be honored in 1992 at the unveiling of Kentucky's Bicentennial stamp, which featured the Home.

There is little space for personal belongings in half of a nursing home room, but I have kept with me all these years my clippings and the manuscripts, in several revisions, of the stories I have written down of my memories. They filled three cartons and two small suitcases stashed about the room. At times, various people encouraged me and helped me to get them organized and to find a publisher for them; they thought it was an interesting life.

Of what am I most proud? I was connected with several "firsts," especially in my Washington career. I think I never let being a woman limit my horizons. In fact, I think there were times when being feminine was much to my advantage.

I knew many fascinating men. Of them all, who really held my heart? Of course, my father, whom I first loved. Sam Conner was a dear man, and had not his untimely death intervened, we might have gotten back together. Dan Talbott launched me into the political world. Harry Byrd was a famous and fascinatingly powerful man when I met him. He dazzled me at first by introducing this country girl to the whirl of Washington society. Joe Sharfsin was intelligent and savvy. MacInnerney was crude, and Goetz was weak.

Though I accepted the limits of my relationship with Jim Farley, I do feel we were twin souls. My love for him was different from that shared with any other man. And if one considers power to be ultimately the most compelling attribute in a man, the one who could give me the most could be none other than Franklin Roosevelt.

In retrospect, would I do some things differently? Probably.

Do I have any regrets? No, none at all.

Index